Cross-Cultural
Research Methods

Cross-Cultural Research Methods

Carol R. Ember and Melvin Ember

A Division of
ROWMAN & LITTLEFIELD PUBLISHERS, INC.
Lanham • Walnut Creek • New York • Oxford

ALTAMIRA PRESS

A Division of Rowman & Littlefield Publishers, Inc.
1630 North Main Street, #367
Walnut Creek, CA 94596
www.altamirapress.com

Rowman & Littlefield Publishers, Inc.
4720 Boston Way
Lanham, MD 20706

12 Hid's Copse Road
Cumnor Hill, Oxford OX2 9JJ, England

British Library Cataloguing in Publication Information Available

Library of Congress Cataloging-in-Publication Data

Ember, Carol R.
 Cross-cultural research methods / Carol R. Ember and Melvin Ember.
  p. cm.
 Includes bibliographical references and index.
 ISBN 0-7425-0426-3 (cloth : alk. paper) — ISBN 0-7425-0427-1 (pbk. : alk. paper)
 1. Cross-cultural studies. I. Ember, Melvin. II. Title.
 GN345.7 .E53 2000
 306'.072—dc21   00-59346

Printed in the United States of America

♾™ The paper used in this publication meets the minimum requirements of American
National Standard for Information Sciences—Permanence of Paper for Printed Library
Materials, ANSI/NISO Z.39.48–1992.

Contents

Preface

This is a "how to" book. We describe and discuss the major principles and methods of cross-cultural research, particularly how to test hypotheses on worldwide samples of cultures. We hope to encourage an increase in such research by showing that it is not hard to do. We have deliberately tried to write the book with a minimum of technical terms to make it easier to read. When we have to use technical terms, we put them in boldface when they first appear, we define them right away, and we include them in the glossary. We take particular pleasure in finding ways to describe complex matters in everyday terms. We hope that we have been able to do so.

We have been doing cross-cultural research for most of our professional lives, on many questions, and we think we have learned how to teach it. We would like to thank many people and the National Science Foundation (NSF) for their advice and support over the years. The NSF supported a conference in 1988 at the Human Relations Area Files (HRAF) on assessing the past and future of cross-cultural research. The participants in that conference suggested that HRAF should apply to NSF to support Summer Institutes in Comparative Anthropological Research to train a new generation of cross-cultural researchers. NSF awarded a three-year grant (for 1991–1993) to HRAF that helped thirty-six anthropologists and other social scientists learn more about cross-cultural research. A second three-year NSF grant to HRAF supported the training of thirty-six other people in 1996–1998. We are grateful to our colleagues, especially Robert L. Munroe, Michael Burton, and Carmella Moore, who taught at the Institutes with Carol Ember. We learned a lot from them and we appreciate their friendship. Questions from and discussion with the Institute participants also helped clarify our thinking. We enjoyed the six summers immensely.

Several other people over the years have encouraged us to write a "how to" book on cross-cultural research, including Burton Pasternak, Daniel Gross, Douglas Schwartz, and Russ Bernard. And last, but not least, we thank Mitch Allen of AltaMira Press for pressuring us to write the book now.

1

The Logic of Cross-Cultural Research

Anthropology tries to understand humans in all their variety. All human populations that have ever existed are of interest to us, from millions of years ago to the present, in all corners of the globe. For a century or more, cultural anthropologists have been painstakingly collecting information about people in widely dispersed places, living for a year or more with people, usually in a very different culture from their own, and describing their way of life in ethnographic books and monographs. Good description is an essential part of science. But it is not enough. Most scientists agree that it is also necessary to arrive at reliably supported explanations of why things are the way they are (Hempel 1965; Nagel 1961). As we shall see, the explanatory part of the enterprise requires comparison.

To compare cultures is not to deny their individual uniqueness. Ethnography and comparative research deal with the same observable characteristics, but they look differently at reality. All snowflakes are unique in the details of their shape, but they are all roughly hexagonal, and they all melt at a temperature above 32° Fahrenheit (at sea level). Ethnography tells us about the unique, what is distinctive about a particular culture; cross-cultural comparison tells us about what is general, what is true for some or many or even all human cultures. If we want to generalize across cultures, how can we move from the particulars of individual ethnographies to the formulation of general (cross-cultural) statements about the similarities and differences of cultures, and what they may be related to?

Without ethnography, to be sure, cross-cultural comparison would be impossible. But without cross-cultural comparison, we could not talk or write about what may be universal and variable about human cultures, and we could not discover why the variation exists. Ethnography and cross-cultural comparison are not contradictory. They inform each other. As focused on the particular as ethnography is, even ethnography is implicitly comparative or cross-cultural. Ethnography employs words, and words are always applicable to more than one instance. It is impossible to describe a particular culture (or anything else, for that matter) without using words that have meanings for others. Why else do we write an article or a book? When you deal in words, you always deal in symbols that transcend an individual person's idiosyncratic, private meanings. That's because every word stands for some *kind* of repeated thing or experience. Words are always comparative. That's why we can talk about and share experiences. If words did not have general meanings, if they referred only to the unique and the private, we could not communicate at all. (The word "communicate" comes from the Latin, "to make common.") Anyone who claims that comparing cultures is not possible because all cultures are unique would have to deny the possibility of all communication. The particulars an ethnographer may notice are often noticed precisely because they exemplify a familiar pattern, or because they contrast with a common pattern. Either way of looking—for uniqueness or similarity—is comparative. Things or events or experiences may not be completely comparable, because they are all individually unique. But if we can use words to describe them, they cannot be completely incomparable.

In everyday parlance, as well as in anthropology, the phrase "cross-cultural" can be used loosely to refer to any kind of comparison of different cultures. Here our meaning is more specific. We focus on systematic comparisons that explicitly aim to answer questions about the incidence, distribution, and causes of cultural variation. (To discover causes or predictors is the most common aim of cross-cultural studies.) Those who call themselves cross-cultural researchers usually employ standard principles of scientific method and research design—random or other sampling that is supposed to be unbiased, reliable, or repeatable measurements so that others can try to replicate our results, statistical evaluation of results so we can know how much confidence we can place in them, and so forth. The relationship between cross-cultural research and the study of a particular culture is analogous to the relationship between epidemiology and the clinical practice of medicine. In ethnographic research and in clinical practice, the primary focus is on the individual case—the patient in medicine, the society or culture in cultural anthropology. Epidemiologists study the characteristics of populations more generally. They look at the incidence and distribution of diseases across populations and they try to understand the causes of those diseases, primarily through correlational analyses of presumed causes and effects. Similarly, cross-cultural researchers are interested in the causes and effects of cultural variation across a wide domain, usually worldwide.

Before we review the assumptions and features of cross-cultural research, and how you can go about doing a cross-cultural study, we think it is a good idea to devote some more space to discussing the unique versus the comparable in the domain of culture. No matter how much space we might devote to the kinds and methods of cross-cultural research, the whole enterprise can be incomprehensible if it is not first understood why cross-cultural comparison is possible—why it is not only good or useful to compare, but also why it is not that hard to do!

UNIQUENESS AND COMPARABILITY

As implied above, there are those who believe that cultures are so diverse and unique that they can only be described in their own terms. From this point of view, comparison is a waste of time, if not wholly illegitimate. The argument is that there are no similarities between cultures, because every culture is unique, and therefore no general statements can be made. But this argument is not correct. If you cannot focus your eyes on two things at the same time, that doesn't mean that you can't focus on two things consecutively. Cross-culturalists do not deny the uniqueness of each culture; uniqueness and similarity are always present, simultaneously. Which you see depends on how you focus.

To illustrate how things can be unique and comparable at the same time, consider the following ethnographic statements about sexuality in three different cultures:[1]

1. The Mae Enga in the Western Highlands of Papua New Guinea believe that "copulation is in itself detrimental to male well-being. Men believe that the vital fluid residing in a man's skin makes it sound and handsome, a condition that determines and reflects his mental vigor and self-confidence. This fluid also manifests itself as his semen. Hence, every ejaculation depletes his vitality, and overindulgence must dull his mind and leave his body permanently exhausted and withered" (Meggitt 1964: 210).
2. "The Nupe men [of Nigeria], certainly, make much of the physically weakening effects of sexual intercourse, and teach the younger generation to husband their strength" (Nadel 1954: 179).
3. "[T]he milk avoidances of the Nilotes [Shilluk of the Sudan] are dependent on fear of contamination associated with the sexual act. . . .

Only small boys herd the cattle and milk them, for once a boy has reached maturity there is the danger that he may have had sexual contact, when if he milked, or handled manure, or even walked among the cattle in their pens, he would cause them to become sterile. . . . If a man has had sexual relations with his wife or another he is considered unclean and does not drink milk until the sun has set the following day" (Seligman and Seligman 1932: 73).

Taken at face value, these three statements about male sexuality are each unique. Indeed, no statement about anything in a particular culture, about sexuality or any other aspect of life, will be exactly like a corresponding statement about another culture. But there are also similarities in these statements that suggest a continuum of variation—a continuum describable as variation in the degree to which males in a society believe that heterosexual sex is harmful to their health. Enga and Nupe males apparently think that heterosexual sex is harmful. It is not so clear what Shilluk males think, because the statement quoted refers to harm to cattle and avoidance of milk, not to the health of males. But suppose we framed the question a different way and asked if people in a particular culture believed that heterosexuality (even with legitimate partners) brought some harm or danger. In regard to this question, we would have to say that all three of the cultures believed that heterosexual sex is harmful.

The important point here is that similarities cannot be seen or recognized until we think in terms of **variables**, qualities or quantities that vary along specified dimensions. Weight is a variable. So are beliefs about heterosexuality as harmful. There is no right or wrong conceptualization of variables; the researcher may choose to focus on any aspect of variation. Once researchers perceive and specify similarity, they can perceive and recognize difference. Measurement—deciding how one case differs from another in terms of some scale—is but a short conceptual step away.

Consider now the following ethnographic statements:

4. For the Cuna of Panama, "the sexual impulse is regarded as needing relief, particularly for males, and as an expression of one's *niga*, a supernatural attribute manifested in potency and strength. On the other hand it is considered debilitating to have sexual relations too often, for this will weaken one's *niga*" (Stout 1947: 39).
5. In regard to the Bedouin of Kuwait: "It [sexual intercourse] is the one great pleasure common to rich and poor alike, and the one moment of forgetfulness in his daily round of troubles and hardships that Badawin [Bedouin] or townsmen can enjoy. Men and women equally love the act, which is said to keep man [sic] young, 'just like riding a mare'" (Dickson 1951: 162).

The Bedouin beliefs contrast most sharply with the beliefs in the other cultures, because heterosexual intercourse appears to be viewed by the Bedouins as purely pleasurable, with no negative associations. The Cuna seem somewhere in the middle. While they view sex as important, they appear to believe that too much is not good. Mixed beliefs are not a problem if the variable is conceptualized as a continuum with gradations. So, in a cross-cultural study conducted by Carol Ember, in which the focus was on a variable labeled "degree of men's fear of sex with women," four scale points were identified: societies with only negative statements (in the ethnography) about heterosexuality were considered high on men's fear of sex with women; those societies with more or less an equal number of negative and positive statements were considered ambivalent; those with *mostly* positive statements were considered relatively low on men's fear of sex with women; and those with *only* positive statements were considered as lacking men's fear of sex with women. While the variable as operationally defined does not capture everything in a culture's beliefs about heterosexuality (in all their uniqueness), it does capture some distinguishable similarities and differences across cultures (C. R. Ember 1978a).

The details of the ethnographic examples quoted above are unique. If we focus on those particulars, we may think that the different cultures are incomparable. But, as these examples also show, if we focus instead on a specified aspect or dimension of the variation, similarities and differences become apparent. By focusing on the variable, we do not lose the uniqueness, we just allow ourselves to perceive the commonalties that are there; we can see how some things are like or different from other things.

THE CROSS-CULTURAL RESEARCH STRATEGY: BASIC ASSUMPTIONS

The most basic assumption of cross-cultural research is that comparison is possible because patterns (kinds of phenomena that occur repeatedly) can be identified. Cross-culturalists believe that all generalizations require testing, no matter how plausible we may think they are. This requirement applies to descriptive generalizations presumed to be true (for example, the presumption that hunter-gatherers are typically peaceful) as well as to presumed relationships or associations (for example, the presumption that hunting is more likely to be associated with patrilocality). As it turns out, both of the presumptions just mentioned are *not* generally true of hunter-gatherers (C. R. Ember 1975, 1978b). It is necessary to test all presumed generalizations or relationships because they may be wrong, and we are entitled (even obliged) to be skeptical about any generalization that has not been supported by an appropriate statistical test. But a test requires comparison: to understand why a particular community or culture is the way it is, we must compare that case with others. Without such a contrast, we have no way of evaluating whether a presumed cause and its apparent effect are associated in a statistically significant way (i.e., that they co-occur more often than you would expect by chance). This is because any single case has an enormous number of traits, and any one or more of them may cause or explain what we are interested in explaining. So we have to test presumed associations comparatively, on a representative sample of cases.

To illustrate our inability to infer an association or relationship from one case, look at figure 1.1. The top part of figure 1.1 shows a square representing one society as observed in the 1950s—the !Kung San of the Kalahari Desert in South Africa. There are very few hunter-gatherers remaining in the world today; the San are one of the most studied of those groups. Indeed, some who have studied them have argued that they represent a rare glimpse at what human life was like before agriculture developed in the world. If we assume that the San are typical hunter-gatherers, we would infer that other features of their life were common in the past. In the box we list some of the features of San life in the 1950s. We might guess that hunter-gatherers tend to be peaceful because the !Kung did not have warfare in the 1950s. But does this necessarily imply that peacefulness is generally associated with hunting and gathering? The answer is no. Just because one case has some features does not mean that most cases have them. While we might attribute the lack of war to hunting and gathering, the real reason(s) might be *any other feature(s)* of the !Kung way of life. Why not argue that the lack of war is related to temporary houses or any other feature listed in the box of observed traits? There are also features, represented by the dotted lines, that we haven't listed. Any or all of those features may be more connected to peacefulness than hunting and gathering. In fact, that is true; a hunting and gathering lifestyle does not generally predict more peacefulness, when you control for other predictors (C. R. Ember and M. Ember 1997). The point here is that there is *no way* to decide which traits in a single society are causally connected to other traits. Every society has an infinite number of describable characteristics and a general (cross-cultural) relationship between one feature and another is impossible to demonstrate on the basis of the one case.

Suppose we decide to compare a hunting-gathering society with an agricultural society. This type of comparison is illustrated by the two boxes in the lower part of figure 1.1. Notice that the agricultural society has war, but the hunting-gathering society does not. Is this better evidence for inferring what causes or predicts war? We would argue not. There are many, many other traits in the agricultural society; we have

A one-case analysis:

Observed traits of one society—the !Kung San in the 1950s

hunters and gatherers   no warfare
small communities   low rainfall
no social stratification   nomadic bands
temporary houses   few possessions
use bows and arrows   share meat
              .   .
              .   .
              .   .

**A hypothetical two-case comparison between a hunting
and gathering group and an agricultural group:**

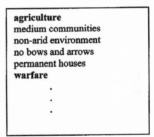

Hunting and Gathering Group   Agricultural Group

hunting and gathering   agriculture
small communities   medium communities
arid environment   non-arid environment
bows and arrows   no bows and arrows
temporary houses   permanent houses
no warfare   **warfare**
              .   .
              .   .
              .   .

**Figure 1.1.   An "Association" of Traits in a One-Case and a Two-Case
Analysis.**

listed just a few. Yes, the agricultural society has warfare, but it also has
medium size communities and permanent settlements and no bows and
arrows. We could just as easily say that one or more of these conditions
may explain the presence of warfare. A two-case comparison is not more
useful than a one-case analysis if we want to demonstrate a cross-cultural
relationship (Campbell 1961: 344). It is only when we compare multiple
cases of hunting-gathering versus agricultural societies, to see if one type
is more likely than the other to have war, that we can begin to see if the
two factors are probably connected. In other words, it is only when we investigate a sample of situations with *and* without the presumed cause that
we can discover a statistically significant association between (or general

co-occurrence of) the presumed cause and effect. And only if we find such an association can we presume that the tested explanation may be correct. We say "may be" because there never is absolute proof of a theory, as we shall see in the next chapter.

To illustrate how larger comparisons help, let us examine the twelve hypothetical cases in table 1.1, some with and some without hunting and gathering. Some of the features that were included in figure 1.1 are listed in a column for each case. (Keep in mind that we have not discussed how the features could be measured.) What we are looking for is whether low warfare seems to be associated with hunting and gathering across a broad spectrum of cases. If low warfare is characteristic of hunter-gatherers, we should see "no warfare" or "low warfare" across the bottom row of the hunter-gatherer cases. And we should see "high warfare" across the bottom of the agricultural cases. The actual pattern in these twelve hypothetical cases does not look that clear. It is hard to tell if warfare is related to hunting and gathering. To make things clearer, it helps to construct what is called a contingency table. A **contingency table** consists of rows displaying variability in one variable and columns displaying variability in a second variable that shows the frequency of cases in each combination of values. What we do to construct such a table (see table 1.2a) is count how many cases have no warfare and hunting and gathering and place that number (two, cases 1 and 2) in the box that intersects the two variables. Then we count how many cases have low warfare and hunting and gathering (there are also two, cases 3 and 5), and we count all of the remaining combinations until we put all twelve of the cases into the table. If we look across the hunting and gathering row (in table 1.2a) we see that four of the six hunting-gathering cases have low or no warfare. And, if we look at the agricultural row, four of the six cases have medium or high warfare. In other words, there is a slight tendency for hunter-gatherers to have less warfare than agriculturalists in this hypothetical table. This tendency is not greater than you would expect by chance, echoing the real cross-cultural results reported in C. R. Ember and M. Ember (1997). However, if we construct a contingency table to look at the relationship between type of subsistence and permanence of settlements from this same hypothetical data-set, the pattern of relationship looks stronger than the one between hunting-gathering and warfare (see table 1.2b). All four of the cases that have temporary houses are hunter-gatherers and all four of the cases that have permanent communities or communities in which people live for many years are agriculturalists. The distribution of cases shown in table 1.2b is unlikely to occur by chance and the contingency table echoes findings from larger samples that hunter-gatherers tend to lack permanent communities (Textor 1967).

Table 1.1. List of Traits in Twelve Hypothetical Cases

Case	Subsistence	Community size	Bows and arrows	Houses	Environment	Warfare
Case 1	hunting and gathering	small communities	bows and arrows	temporary houses	non-arid environment	no warfare
Case 2	hunting and gathering	small communities	no bows and arrows	seasonal permanent houses	non-arid environment	no warfare
Case 3	hunting and gathering	medium communities	bows and arrows	temporary houses	arid environment	low frequency warfare
Case 4	hunting and gathering	small communities	bows and arrows	temporary houses	arid environment	high frequency warfare
Case 5	hunting and gathering	small-medium communities	no bows and arrows	seasonal permanent houses	non-arid environment	low frequency warfare
Case 6	hunting and gathering	small communities	no bows and arrows	temporary houses	arid environment	medium frequency warfare
Case 7	agriculture	small communities	bows and arrows	seasonal permanent houses	non-arid environment	high frequency warfare
Case 8	agriculture	medium communities	no bows and arrows	houses lived in for many years	arid environment	medium frequency warfare
Case 9	agriculture	medium communities	no bows and arrows	houses lived in for many years	non-arid environment	low frequency warfare
Case 10	agriculture	small-medium communities	no bows and arrows	seasonal permanent houses	arid environment	medium frequency warfare
Case 11	agriculture	large communities	no bows and arrows	permanent houses	non-arid environment	no warfare
Case 12	agriculture	large communities	no bows and arrows	permanent houses	arid environment	high frequency warfare

Table 1.2a. **Hypothetical Contingency Table Showing the Relationship between Hunting-Gathering (versus Agriculture) and Frequency of Warfare**

	no warfare	*low warfare*	*medium warfare*	*high warfare*
hunting-gathering	2	2	1	1
agriculture	1	1	2	2

Table 1.2b. **Hypothetical Contingency Table Showing the Relationship between Hunting-Gathering (versus Agriculture) and Permanence of Housing**

	temporary houses	*seasonal permanent houses*	*live for many years in the same community*	*permanent houses*
hunting-gathering	4	2		
agriculture		2	2	2

The fundamental assumption of a cross-cultural study is that if a theory or hypothesis has merit, the presumed causes and effects should be significantly and strongly associated synchronically (J. W. M. Whiting 1954). A **synchronic association** involves variables that are measured for each sample case for more or less the same time period, as if we were examining ethnographic "snapshots," each capturing a culture at a particular time (and usually in a particular locality). Regardless of the different time foci for the sample cases, a significant result should be obtained if there is a systematic relationship between or among the measured variables. A significant association is one that would hardly ever occur just by chance (see chapter 8). A strong association means that one variable predicts another to a high degree. Thus the cross-cultural research strategy provides a way to falsify hypotheses that have no predictive value, and hence presumably no causal value.

Cross-culturalists do not believe that cross-cultural research is the only way to test theory about cultural variation. However, such research is viewed as one of the more important ways to test theory, if only because cross-cultural research (if it involves a worldwide sample of cases) provides the most generalizable results of any kind of social scientific research. (More on this point later.) Most cross-culturalists believe in the multimethod approach to testing theory; that is, they believe that worldwide cross-cultural tests should be supplemented (when possible and not impossibly costly) by studies of variation within one or more particular field sites (comparisons of individuals, households, communities) as well as within particular regions (e.g., North America, Southeast Asia). Theories may also be testable experimentally and by computer simulations, as well as by examining historical and cross-historical data.

Before we discuss the advantages and disadvantages of the various kinds of comparative and cross-cultural research, let us first provide a little historical background.

HISTORY OF CROSS-CULTURAL RESEARCH

The first cross-cultural study was published in 1889 by Edward B. Tylor. In that study, Tylor attempted to relate marital residence and the reckoning of kinship to other customs such as joking and avoidance relationships. But, perhaps because of Francis Galton's objection to Tylor's presentation—see the "Discussion" section at the end of Tylor's paper—cross-cultural research was hardly undertaken for the next forty years. (What has come to be called **"Galton's Problem"** was about whether the cases in Tylor's study were all independent—we return to this issue later.) Cross-cultural research started to become more popular in the 1930s and 1940s, at the Institute of Human Relations at Yale. The person who led this rebirth was anthropologist George Peter Murdock (1897–1985). Murdock had obtained his Ph.D. (1925) at Yale in a combined sociology/anthropology department that called itself the "Science of Society" (its comparative perspective was established by its founder, William Graham Sumner).

Perhaps the major boost to cross-cultural studies was the development by the Yale group of an organized collection of ethnographic information (first called the "Cross-Cultural Survey," the precursor of what we now call the "Human Relations Area Files Collection of Ethnography") that could be used by scholars to compare the cultures of the world. In the early part of the twentieth century, Sumner had compiled voluminous materials on peoples throughout the world, but his compilation suffered from being limited to subjects in which he was personally interested. Later, at the Institute of Human Relations, the group of social and behavioral scientists led by Murdock (including psychologists, physiologists, sociologists, and anthropologists) set out to improve upon Sumner's work by developing the Cross-Cultural Survey. The aim was to foster comparative research on humans in all their variety so that explanations of human behavior would not be culture-bound.

The first step was to develop a classification system to organize the descriptive information on different cultures. This category system became the *Outline of Cultural Materials* (the most recent revision is Murdock et al. 2000). The next step in building the files was to select well-described cases and to index the ethnography on them, paragraph by paragraph and sometimes even sentence by sentence, for the subject matters covered on a page. Since the aim was to file information by subject category to facilitate comparison, and since a page usually contained more than one type of information, the extracts of ethnographic information were typed using carbon paper to make the number of copies needed (corresponding to the number of topics covered); carbon paper was used because the Cross-Cultural Survey ante-dated photocopying and computers. In 1946, the directorship of the Cross-Cultural Survey was turned over to Clellan S. Ford, who undertook to transform it into a consortium of universities so that the comparative data could be available at other universities in addition to Yale. In 1949, first five then eight universities joined together to sponsor a not-for-profit consortium called the Human Relations Area Files, Incorporated (HRAF), with headquarters in New Haven. (The name was derived from the Institute of Human Relations, where the consortium was first housed.) Over the years, the HRAF consortium added member institutions, and more and more cultures were added to the HRAF collection. Member institutions in the early days received the annual installments of information as photocopies. Later, the preferred medium became microfiche. Since 1994 the member institutions in the HRAF consortium have accessed the collection electronically, at first on CD-ROM and now on the World Wide Web. The technological changes over time have allowed the full-text HRAF Collection of Ethnography to become more and more widely accessible and more and more efficiently searchable. New cases are added each year. And now, when old cases are added to the eHRAF, they are almost always extensively updated; an updated case, if there has been recent fieldwork on it, may now have nearly 50 percent new material. (For more information on the evolution of HRAF as an organization and as collections of data for cross-cultural research, see M. Ember 1997.)

The accessibility that HRAF provides to indexed full-text ethnographic information has undoubtedly increased the number of cross-cultural studies. Considering just worldwide comparisons (which are the most common type of cross-cultural study), in the years between 1889 and 1947 there were only ten worldwide cross-cultural studies. In the following twenty years there were 127. And in the next twenty years (ending in 1987) there were 440 (C. R. Ember and Levinson 1991: 138). Now, there may be nearly 1,000 worldwide cross-cultural studies in the published literature. For various reasons (see M. Ember 1997), this trend is likely to continue. Indeed, we can expect the rate of comparative research to increase enormously, now that the electronic HRAF databases (eHRAF Ethnography and eHRAF Archaeology) are available on the Web to institutions around the world.

TYPES OF CROSS-CULTURAL COMPARISON

Cross-cultural comparisons vary along four dimensions: (1) geographical scope of the comparison—whether the sample is worldwide or is limited to a geographic area (e.g., a region such as North America); (2) size of the sample—two-case comparisons, small-scale comparisons (fewer than ten cases), and larger comparisons; (3) whether the data used are primary (collected by the investigator in various field sites explicitly for a comparative study) or secondary (collected by others and found by the comparative researcher in ethnographies, censuses, and histories); and (4) whether the data on a given case pertain to (or date from) just one time period (this is a **"synchronic comparison"** of cases) or two or more time periods (this is a **"diachronic comparison"**). While all combinations of these four dimensions are technically possible, some combinations are quite rare. Worldwide cross-cultural comparisons using secondary synchronic data (one "ethnographic present" for each sample case) are the most common in anthropology.

Comparative research is not just done in anthropology. Worldwide studies using ethnographic data are increasingly done by evolutionary biologists, sociologists, political scientists, and others. Cross-cultural psychologists often compare people in different cultures. And various kinds of social scientists compare across nations.

The cross-national comparison is narrower than the worldwide cross-cultural comparison, because the results of a cross-national comparison are generalizable only to a limited range of cross-cultural variation, namely, that which encompasses only the complex societies (usually multicultural nation-states) of recent times. In contrast, the results of a cross-cultural study are generalizable to all types of society, from hunter-gatherers with populations in the hundreds or a few thousand, to agrarian state societies with populations in the millions, to modern nation-states with populations in the hundreds of millions. Cross-national studies by political scientists, economists, and sociologists generally use secondary data for their samples of nations. But the data are not generally ethnographic in origin; that is, the measures used are not generally based on cultural information collected by anthropologists or other investigators in the field. Rather the data used in cross-national comparisons are generally based on censuses and other nationally collected statistics (crime rates, gross national product, etc.), often as documented over time. Cross-cultural psychologists generally collect their own (primary) data, but their comparisons tend to be the most limited of all; often only two cultures are compared (the investigator's own and one other).

Cross-historical studies are still comparatively rare in anthropology (but see Naroll, Bullough and Naroll 1974). Few worldwide or even within-region cross-cultural studies have employed data on a given case that come from or pertain to more than one time period. Some cross-national studies have been cross-historical studies as well. Such studies can be done by sociologists, political scientists, and economists because there are accessible historical databases for nations. Since primary data are so hard and expensive to collect, it is hardly surprising that primary comparisons are likely to be small in scale. If you have to collect your data yourself, going to several places to do so takes a lot of time and money. Large-scale comparisons, which almost always rely on secondary data (collected or assembled previously by others), are generally much less expensive. So worldwide cross-cultural studies are generally more cost effective, as well as more generalizable, than other kinds of comparative research.

Now, particularly with the development of HRAF's Collection of Archaeology, two kinds of archaeological comparisons will become more likely. One type, which is analogous to worldwide cross-cultural comparisons, will be worldwide archaeological comparisons using "snapshots" of particular times and places in prehistory. Each archaeological tradition (e.g., Classic Maya) becomes a case. A second type of archaeological comparison will be analogous to cross-historical comparison: researchers will use changes over time to test causal or developmental theories.

Let us turn now to the advantages and disadvantages of the different types of cross-cultural comparison. Our discussion compares the different types with particular regard to the two major goals of scientific studies—theory formulation and theory testing.

Advantages and Disadvantages of the Different Types of Comparison

Worldwide cross-cultural comparisons have two major advantages, compared with other types of comparative research (M. Ember 1991). The major one, as we have already noted, is that the statistical conclusions drawn from a worldwide comparison of all types of society are probably applicable to the entire ethnographic record, assuming that the sample is more or less free of bias. (See chapter 6 on sampling.) In contrast to the results of a within-region comparison, which may or may not be applicable to other regions, and in contrast to the results of a cross-national comparison, which may or may not be applicable to the ethnographic record, the results of a worldwide cross-cultural comparison are probably applicable to most if not all regions and most if not all types of societies in the ethnographic record. Thus, other things being equal, the worldwide type of cross-cultural comparison has a better chance than other types of comparison of coming close to the goal of knowing that a finding or an observed relationship has nearly universal validity, which is consistent with the general scientific goal of more and more comprehensive explanations. (Most cross-cultural studies under-sample modern industrial societies, but this deficiency will disappear as the ethnographic record increasingly includes the results of ethnographic field studies in industrial countries.)

In addition to the advantage of greater generalizability of results, the worldwide cross-cultural comparison offers another advantage: it maximizes the amount or range of variation in the variables investigated. This advantage of more variation may make the difference between a useful and a useless study. Without variation, it is impossible to see a relationship between variables. So, if a researcher uses data from a single society, a single region, or even from the recent historical record for nation-states, there may be little or no variation to relate to other things. Even if there is some variation, it may be at just one end of the spectrum of variation. So we may think a relationship is positive or negative, because that is all we can observe in one region or in one type of society, but the relationship may be curvilinear in the world, as J. W. M. Whiting (1954: 524–25) noted nearly fifty years ago. For example, this is the result when we plot socio-economic inequality against level of economic development in the ethnographic record. There is little socio-economic inequality in hunter-gatherer societies (H/G), there is a lot of inequality in preindustrial agrarian societies, and inequality is lower again—but hardly absent—in modern industrial societies (M. Ember, C. R. Ember, and Russett 1997). If we were to restrict our purview only to industrial societies, it would appear that more equality goes with higher levels of economic development (see line B in figure 1.2). But if we looked only at preindustrial societies, it would appear that more equality goes with *lower* levels of economic development (see line A in figure 1.2). Thus, if we want to be sure about the nature or shape of a relationship, we have to conduct a worldwide cross-cultural comparison. Otherwise, we run the risk of being misled. A worldwide cross-cultural sample, because it represents the maximum range of variation in the ethnographic record, is the most reliable way to discover exactly how variables are related in the entire range of human societies. If you want to say something about humans in general, there is no substitute for a worldwide cross-cultural study.

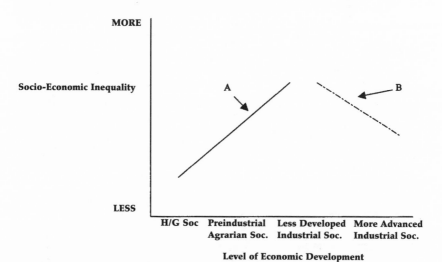

Figure 1.2. A Simplified View of the Relationship between Degree of Socioeconomic Inequality and Level of Economic Development.

These same advantages, by the way, pertain to worldwide cross-archaeological studies. Cross-archaeological studies, which are likely to be done more frequently (now that eHRAF Archaeology facilitates them), should produce generalizations that are true for all periods of prehistory.

But a cross-cultural study might be unsuccessful. And then the researcher could be stuck. A researcher is unlikely to know much about individual societies when comparing a lot of societies from different parts of the world. If a tested explanation turns out to be supported, the lack of detailed knowledge about the sample cases is not much of a problem. If, however, the cross-cultural test is disconfirming, it may be difficult to come up with an alternative explanation without knowing more about the particular cases. More familiarity with the cases may help in formulating a revised or new theory that could be tested and supported (Johnson 1991). Because most anthropologists have regional specialties, the regional comparativist is likely to know a lot about each society in a within-region comparison. So narrowing the scope of a comparative study to a single region may mean that you can know more about the cases, and therefore you may be more likely to come up with a revised theory if your first tests are unsuccessful. Of course, restricting the study to a region does not allow you to discover that the results of the comparison apply to the whole world. (For further discussion see Burton and White 1991.) Even a regional comparativist may not know all the cases in the region; that depends mostly on the size of the region. If the region is as large as North America, the comparativist is likely to know less about the cases than if the region studied is the American Southwest. And if you need to look at a sample of the rest of the world to discover how generalizable your results are, you might as well do a worldwide study in the first place!

It should be noted that the objective of large-scale within-region comparisons (using data on all or most of the societies in the region) is usually different from the objective of a worldwide cross-cultural study (Burton and White 1991). Using large numbers of cultural traits, within-region comparativists generally try to arrive at classifications of cultures in order to make inferences about processes of diffusion and historical ancestry. Instead of trying to see how cultural traits may be causally related to each other, within-region comparativists are generally more interested in trying to see how the cultures in the region are related to each another. But some regional comparativists are interested in pursuing both objectives at the same time (Jorgensen 1974). The importance of looking at worldwide as well as regional samples, especially if you are interested in relationships between or among variables, is indicated by the following discussion.

Consider the discrepancy between the findings of Driver and Massey (1957) and the findings of M. Ember and C. R. Ember (1971) and Divale

(1974) with regard to the relationship between division of labor by gender and where couples live after they marry. Driver and Massey found support in aboriginal North America for Murdock's (1949: 203ff.) idea that division of labor by gender determined matrilocal versus patrilocal residence, but the Embers (and Divale) found no support for this idea in worldwide samples. The Embers found that the relationship varies from region to region. In North America there is a significant relationship, but in other regions the relationship is not significant. And in Oceania, there is a trend in the opposite direction; matrilocal societies there are more likely to have men doing more in primary subsistence activities. What is it about the variation from region to region that might account for differences in the direction of the relationship in different regions? C. R. Ember (1975) found that the relationship between a male-dominated division of labor and patrilocal residence did hold for hunter-gatherers; hence she suggested that the frequent occurrence of hunter-gatherers in North America (cf. Witkowski n.d.) may account for the statistically significant relationship between a male-dominant division of labor and patrilocal residence in North America.

Fred Eggan (1954) advocated small-scale regional comparisons, which he called "controlled comparisons," because he thought they would make it easier to rule out the possible effects of similarity in history, geography, and language. His presumption was that the researcher could readily discern what accounts for some aspect of cultural variation within the region if history, geography, and language were held constant. However, the similarity of cases within a region may be a major drawback. A single region may not show sufficient variability in the aspect of culture the researcher is trying to explain (as well as in the presumed causes). Unless a substantial number of the cases lack what you are trying to explain, it would be difficult or impossible to discern what the phenomenon at issue may be related to. For example, suppose that almost all the cases in a region have beliefs about sexual intercourse being harmful. It would be difficult or nearly impossible to be able to figure out what such beliefs were related to, because you could not tell which of the other regularly occurring practices or beliefs in the region might explain the sexual beliefs. Only if some cases lack what you are trying to explain might you see that the hypothetical causes are also generally absent when the presumed effect is absent. Thus, unless there is sufficient variation in all possibly relevant variables, the controlled comparison strategy is a poor choice for testing theory. Obviously, the controlled comparison is also a poor choice for describing the worldwide incidence of something (unless the region focused on is the only universe of interest). While the strategy of controlled comparison may seem analogous to controls in psychology and sociology (which hold some possible causes, and their effects, constant), the resemblance is only superficial. For psychologists and sociologists typically eliminate certain kinds of variation (e.g., in socioeconomic class, religion, ethnicity, or gender) only when they have prior empirical reasons to think that these factors partially predict the variable they are trying to explain. In contrast, those who do controlled comparisons in the anthropological sense usually only presume, but do not know, that common history, language, or geography has made a difference. If researchers are not really controlling for predictors when they do a controlled comparison, they are not necessarily getting any closer to the causal reality by restricting their study to a particular region.

A decision to collect primary data, in the field, is necessary if the researcher is interested in topics that are hardly (if ever) covered in the ethnographic record. This was the major reason John and Beatrice Whiting (see, e.g., B. B. Whiting 1963), who were interested in children's behavior and what it was related to, decided they had to collect new data in the field for the comparative study that came to be known as the Six Cultures project. Many aspects of socialization (such as particular practices of the mother) were not typically described in ethnographies. Similarly, researchers interested in internal psychological states (such as sex-identity, self-esteem, happiness) could not find out about them from ethnographies, and therefore would need to collect the data themselves, in the field. How time is allocated to various activities is another, nonpsychological example of information that is also not generally covered in ethnographies, or not in sufficient detail. (Of course, once such data are collected, other researchers can use them as secondary data.) Although it may always seem preferable to collect primary data (as opposed to secondary data), because the researcher then is very likely to collect the particular kinds of data sought, the logistics of cross-cultural comparisons using primary data are formidable in time and expense. And the task of maintaining comparability of measures across sites is difficult (R. L. Munroe and R. Munroe 1991a). So, if a researcher has reason for thinking that something like the needed information is already available in ethnographies, a comparison using secondary data is more economical than comparative fieldwork in two or more places. But comparative fieldwork may be the only viable choice when the information needed is not otherwise available. (See box 1.1 for a review of how to decide which kind of cross-cultural comparison is needed.)

Similarly, although it may seem preferable to use diachronic data (history) to test the temporal ordering implied in causal theories, diachronic data are not often readily available. One reason is that most societies studied by cultural anthropologists lacked native writing, so there are usually no historical documents that one could use to measure variables for an earlier time. The alternative is to reconstruct the situation in a prior time

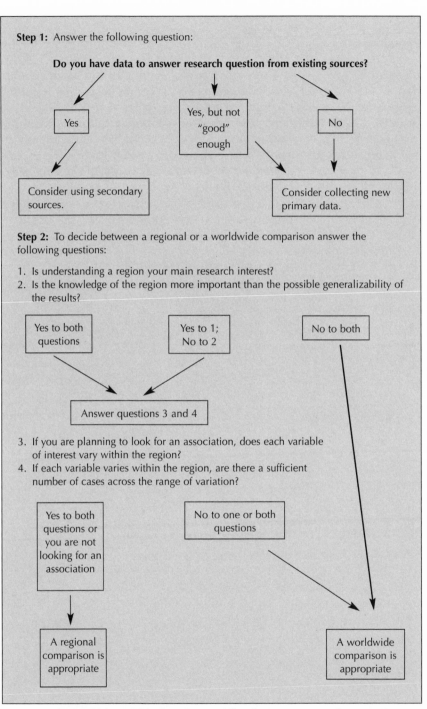

Step 1: Answer the following question:

Do you have data to answer research question from existing sources?

Yes

Yes, but not "good" enough

No

Consider using secondary sources.

Consider collecting new primary data.

Step 2: To decide between a regional or a worldwide comparison answer the following questions:

1. Is understanding a region your main research interest?
2. Is the knowledge of the region more important than the possible generalizability of the results?

Yes to both questions

Yes to 1; No to 2

No to both

Answer questions 3 and 4

3. If you are planning to look for an association, does each variable of interest vary within the region?
4. If each variable varies within the region, are there a sufficient number of cases across the range of variation?

Yes to both questions or you are not looking for an association

No to one or both questions

A regional comparison is appropriate

A worldwide comparison is appropriate

Box 1.1.   Suggested Decision Tree for Deciding between Types of Comparisons

period on the basis of oral history and the occasional documents left by travelers, traders, and other visitors. But such reconstructions are notoriously subject to biases. A second reason it is difficult to find diachronic data is that different ethnographers have different substantive interests, and so the different ethnographers who may have worked in the same place at different times may not have collected information on the same variables. For these reasons, most cross-culturalists think it is more efficient to test causal theories with synchronic data first. If a theory has merit, the presumed causes and effects should generally be associated synchronically. Only if they are should we then try to make a diachronic or cross-historical test. It does not make sense to try to see if the presumed causes antedated the presumed effects unless we see first that the synchronic results show correlation. Diachronic data should become increasingly available as the ethnographic record expands with updating, so we should see more cross-historical studies in the future.

NOTE

1. The following example originally appeared in C. R. Ember and M. Ember (1998).

2

The Research Question

Research projects work best if the researcher can state *a clear, one-sentence question* before starting. Framing the question is often the hardest part of the research process. Why is it so hard? For one thing, the one sentence requires you to focus your interest. A good research question also has to be practical. There is no point in asking a question that you can't expect to answer in a reasonable time frame.

Finding a good question is kind of like Goldilocks's search: she tries a lot of things and they are either too hot or too cold, too hard or too soft. A good research question must be somewhere in the middle: *not too hard, but not too easy, to answer; not too large a question and not too small*. Here are some questions that are too large: What is the meaning of life? Why does culture change? How do females differ from males?

Some of the questions that are too large are not likely to be answerable with social science research. Questions about culture change or gender differences are too large. Which of an infinite number of aspects of culture change or gender difference should we focus on? Without a focus on a smaller aspect of culture change or a smaller set of gender differences, questions that are too large would take more than a lifetime to answer. But it is sometimes hard to say whether a question is too large. It depends on whether or not you see a practical way to answer the question. And that is part of the art of research—seeing or intuiting what is possible.

Here are some questions that are too small: Why do people in Society X make pottery with a unique design? Why do some societies make wooden war clubs? The first question is too small because it is not a general question; it refers only to a single case with a unique feature. If you try to answer a question about some uniqueness, the answer is likely to be trivial or not informative. For example, you could say that the Society X people have this unique design because it is customary, but this answer is an uninformative tautology. It merely says that they have this design because they had this design before. You might invoke a historical explanation: a particular person invented this design and others copied it. But this kind of answer would not explain why the unique design, but not others, was liked and emulated. The second question about wooden war clubs is not so particularistic: many societies have had wooden (and variable) war clubs. However, we would argue that even this question is too small and not as theoretically interesting as other questions about war or technology. So let's widen the focus a bit. Broader questions that could be successfully researched are: What predicts hand-to-hand combat? Why do some societies fight more than others? We ourselves conducted cross-cultural research on the last question (C. R. Ember and M. Ember 1992a, 1992b; C. R. Ember, M. Ember, and Russett 1992; C. R. Ember, Russett, and M. Ember 1993). More general questions such as these can have general answers, and that is what makes research on them more interesting potentially— research might provide answers that fit many situations. General answers to general questions are more informative or explanatory.

TYPES OF COMPARATIVE QUESTIONS

The type of question asked largely determines the nature of the research, including what type of sample should be used, at least some of the variables to measure, and sometimes the type of statistical analysis. We can group questions into four major groups: (1) *descriptive*; (2) *causal*; (3) *consequence*; and (4) *nondirectional relational*. If you know you are interested in a particular type of phenomenon, but you are not sure which type of question you want to frame, it usually helps to try to frame at least one of each type and then ask yourself if you would be happy doing that type of study. We ourselves almost always frame causal or why questions, but other researchers have other preferences.

1. *Descriptive questions* usually deal with the prevalence or frequency of a trait. Examples are: How common is the belief that sex is dangerous to one's health? How common is it for a society to allow polygyny? Are peaceful societies common? Is the custom of marriage universal?

2. *Causal questions* seek answers about the causes of a trait or custom. Examples are: Why do some societies have the belief that heterosex-

ual sex is harmful? Why do some societies insist on monogamous marriage, whereas most allow polygyny? Why is war very frequent in some societies and less frequent in others? Why is marriage a cultural universal?[1]

3. *Consequence questions* ask about effects of a particular trait or custom. This kind of question may be phrased broadly: What are the effects of growing up in a society with a great deal of war? Or a consequence question may be phrased much more specifically: What is the effect of polygyny on fertility?

4. *Nondirectional relational questions* ask whether two traits are related or not, without implying cause or consequence. Examples are: Is there a relationship between type of marriage and level of fertility? Is more war associated with more socialization for aggression in children? Do hunter-gatherers share food more often than food producers? Are males more aggressive than females?

Question types 2 through 4 are relational questions. That is, they ask how traits are related to other traits. Figure 2.1 diagrams the different types of relational questions. Causality is diagrammed with an arrow. A single-headed arrow indicates the direction of causality. A causal question has at least one trait to be explained (the **dependent variable**); the **independent variable**(s) are the presumed causes. (If you find the terms dependent and independent variable confusing, think of independent as free to vary and the dependent variable as not free to vary because it *depends* on some other trait.) A consequence question has a clear independent variable, but the dependent variables may or may not be specified. A double-headed arrow signifies that the direction of causality is not implied.

We said above that the choice of question usually tells you a great deal about what to do next, although as we will see, some questions tell you more than others. Formulating the descriptive question makes most of what you have to do next quite clear. If you want to get an answer to the descriptive question, you know you need to measure the trait in question for a sample that adequately represents the universe of cases to which you want to generalize your results. Thus, the phrasing of the question usually implies the units of analysis (cases) and the scope of the cases to be sampled. Compare the following descriptive questions:

1. How many women in the world today are married polygynously?
2. How many societies allow polygyny?
3. How many societies commonly have polygyny?
4. How many countries in Africa have 20 percent or more of the men married polygynously?

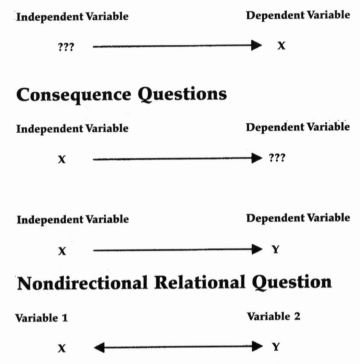

Casual Question

Independent Variable	Dependent Variable
??? ⟶	X

Consequence Questions

Independent Variable	Dependent Variable
X ⟶	???

Independent Variable	Dependent Variable
X ⟶	Y

Nondirectional Relational Question

Variable 1	Variable 2
X ⟷	Y

Figure 2.1.   Types of Relational Questions.

The units of analysis in questions 1 through 4 are individual women, societies, societies, and countries, respectively. A worldwide sample is needed to answer questions 1 through 3, while a regional sample is needed for question 4. All of the questions require defining polygyny, but question 2, in contrast to the others, requires attention to cultural rules rather than actual marriage practices.

Of the four types of questions, the causal or "why" question is the most challenging because it rarely specifies what the researcher needs to do to answer the question. (As shown in figure 2.1, a consequence question could also be unspecific or open-ended; the possible outcomes may not be specified in advance.) The consequence and nondirectional relational questions usually specify a set of concrete things to look at. If you want to know whether type of marriage has an effect on or is related to fertility, then you know you need to measure both variables (type of marriage and fertility). But an open-ended causal (or consequence) question does not tell the researcher exactly *where* to look for causes (or effects). The only thing specified in the open-ended causal question is the dependent variable (the variable to be explained); the only thing specified in the open-ended consequence question is the independent variable (the variable that may have effects). Exactly which variables may be causes or effects is something the investigator has to decide on, often as suggested by some theory (C. R. Ember and M. Ember 1988: 5–6; 1996a).

We ourselves like to think of the causal question as analogous to the format of a detective story. After a crime is committed the detective may know a lot about the crime, but not "whodunit" or why. Finding the solution usually entails theorizing about suspects and their possible motives and opportunities, eliminating the implausible possibilities, and concluding who is probably the culprit. Similarly, in science, the pursuit of causes involves the testing of alternative explanations or theories that specify why something is the way it is or how it came to be that way. The researcher who chooses to investigate a causal question needs to identify plausible explanations or theories that could be tested, and to decide on a strategy (for collecting and analyzing data) that could falsify or disconfirm the tested explanations. Although these requirements may suggest that the researcher who searches for causes needs to act differently as compared with other kinds of researchers, this is not really the case, as we shall see (cf. C. R. Ember and M. Ember 1988: 5–6; 1996b).

In point of fact, most tests of causal or consequence theories rely on nondirectional tests of relationships. That fact should not deter researchers from thinking theoretically. As we will see in chapter 3, theory is critical to a well-designed study.

NOTE

1. A question about a universal custom is difficult to investigate unless you deal with it in a larger domain that has some variation. This is why we decided to conduct a cross-species study of mating; some species have male-female bonding (marriage) whereas others do not (M. Ember and C. R. Ember 1983).

3

Theories and Hypotheses

Underlying most research questions are ideas, implicit or explicit, about how and why things are the way they are. Consider a descriptive question like "How prevalent is war among hunter-gatherers?" The question may be asked because some well-known hunter-gatherers, such as the !Kung San of the Kalahari Desert in South Africa, are described as peaceful (in the 1950s and '60s). Indeed, many anthropologists would like to believe that simpler societies have less war than more complex (state) societies. To answer a descriptive question, it is probably not necessary to spell out the implicit assumptions behind the question, but we would argue that it would be beneficial to do so. For one thing, the exercise of spelling out hidden assumptions might lead you to change your mind about what to investigate and how. Suppose you realized, with reflection, that hunter-gatherers may or may not have less war than complex societies. Wouldn't it be good to find out, by comparing hunter-gatherers with other types of societies? Designing a study to do that might also lead you to reevaluate what you mean by complexity. Do you mean the presence or absence of food production, or do you mean that communities or local groups are large and contain various kinds of specialists? And, if you do decide to compare hunter-gatherers with other types of societies, you would probably need to adopt a definition of war that would pertain to all kinds of societies. With a little more reflection, you might stop and ask yourself *why* you expect hunter-gatherers to fight less. Is it because they don't have much property, or is it because they don't suffer as much from famine and food shortages, or is it because they live in less densely populated territories? Could there be other reasons that you have not thought about (cf. C. R. Ember and M. Ember 1997)? So spelling out your assumptions and the reasons for your expectations can clarify your theorizing and help you derive hypotheses that could be tested.

Naturally, in any scholarly research there is the need to find out what previous researchers have presented by way of evidence and what if any reasons they give for their expectations. But it is always instructive to try to think about what *you think* before you do a literature review. Sometimes naïveté pays off. You might get an idea that others haven't thought about. That doesn't mean that you can ignore what others have said, but if you don't think about why you have your ideas, you may be so intimidated by what established scholars think that you give up on your own ideas prematurely. It is one thing to recognize other opinions. It is another thing to let them deter you from your own research.

When we start to think about why things may work the way they do or how something affects something else, we begin to get closer to an understanding of what we mean when we talk about theory. A theory is one kind of explanation that scientists strive for. The other kind is an association (relationship) or law. Associations may or may not exist; but we can test for them. Theories are more general and not completely testable, but they could explain associations.

The associational way of explaining something (an observation, an action, a custom, a variable) is to say how it conforms to a general principle or relationship.[1] So to explain why the water left outside in the basin froze last night, we say that it was cold last night and that water freezes at 32° Fahrenheit (at sea level). The statement that water solidifies (becomes ice) at 32° Fahrenheit is a statement of relationship or **association** between two variables. In this case, variation in the state of water (liquid versus solid) is related to variation in the temperature of the air (above versus at or below 32° Fahrenheit). The truth of the relationship is suggested by repeated observations (tests). In the physical sciences, such associations are called **laws** when they are accepted as true by most scientists. Lawlike generalizations are explanations for particular events; they allow us to predict what will happen in the future or to understand something that has happened regularly in the past. In the social sciences, associations are statistical or probabilistic; that is, we say that two or more variables tend to be related in a predictable way, which means that there are usually some exceptions. Examples are: Societies with towns and cities tend to have agriculture; societies lacking permanent settlements tend to have fewer household possessions; societies with plow agriculture tend to have men doing relatively more agricultural work than women.

But usually we are not content with lawlike generalizations as explanations. Why does lowering temperature turn the water from a liquid state into a solid? Why does plow agriculture decrease the relative time women and men devote to agriculture? Here's where theories come in. **Theories** are explanations of laws and statistical associations. Theories almost always include some concepts that are, at least at the moment, not directly verifiable (Nagel 1961: 85–89). That's one reason we call them "theoretical"! Let us consider the following association—boys tend to be more aggressive than girls. This association is widely accepted because it is supported by comparative research, e.g., the Six Cultures project (B. B. Whiting and Edwards 1963) and the Munroes' Four Cultures Project (R. L. Munroe et al. 2000), as well as by various within-culture studies. Different researchers have different ideas about *why* this association exists. Some researchers believe that the consistent difference between boys and girls is rooted in some biological difference between boys and girls; others believe that the difference is attributable to differential upbringing. Either premise (that biology or social learning causes the difference) is theoretical. The supposed causal connections are not empirically verifiable. Even in experiments where the observer is manipulating the supposed cause and then observing the supposed effect, there is always the possibility that something else was responsible for the effect. Associations, on the other hand, are verifiable—if they are supported repeatedly, we call them laws.

The theories we mentioned about the causes of gender difference in aggression are very simple. Even so, we think it is important to try to analyze their logic. Doing so may allow us to see that the premises do not necessarily imply what we think they imply, or that the theory needs to be spelled out more. We have to try to specify why we think X causes or leads to Y.

Let us consider two versions of the biological theory of sex differences in aggression.

Theory 1
Assumption 1: A biological difference between the genders causes boys to be more aggressive than girls.
Implication or prediction: Boys will tend to be more aggressive than girls.

What is the point of stating a simple theory like that? We think it is important because it allows you to see flaws in the logic of the theory. In this case, the logic is clear. If a biological difference causes boys to be more aggressive than girls, it is logical to conclude that boys will tend to be more aggressive. The cause should generally be associated with the effect. However, stating the simple assumption pushes us to ask more questions. What it is about the biology that creates the difference? Do boys generally have more of a particular hormone than girls? Is there some genetic difference on the Y chromosome? If the difference is biological in some way, why would some boys be less aggressive than some girls? Some of these questions about theory have led to important lines of research. For example, one biological difference between males and females is that males have more circulating androgen. Some investigators thought that different amounts of androgen cause different amounts of aggression. Spelling out the reasoning leads to additional predictions.

Theory 2
Assumption 1: Androgen increases the likelihood of aggression.
Assumption 2: Males generally have more androgen than females.
Implication or prediction 1: Males will be more aggressive than females.
Implication or prediction 2: Individuals with higher levels of androgen will be more aggressive.

Notice that this more specific theory makes two predictions. (Incidentally, we call such predictions *hypotheses*.) **Hypotheses** posit relationships between variables that ought to be true if the theory is true. Hypotheses are actually the means by which we test theory. If the conclusion logically stems from the premises or assumptions, but the conclusion is not verified, researchers should be skeptical about the theory. With regard to Theory 2 (about androgen), prediction 2 was not verified by research, at least with regard to circulating levels of androgen. In fact, the results from various studies are equivocal. This situation led researchers to consider a revised theory that androgen produced by male fetuses early in pregnancy increases the likelihood of aggression by males later in life. The results of various studies are more consistent with this revised theory.[2]

Notice too that if we had no theory, only an association, all we would know is that boys tend to be more aggressive than girls. We could not enhance our understanding any more than that. Only if we try to state a theory, no matter how simple at first, and then try to obtain evidence to see if a prediction is correct, may we enhance our understanding. One of the important payoffs from theorizing is that it can suggest new tests to answer new questions.

WHY THEORIES CANNOT BE PROVEN

The important thing to understand about theories is that they cannot be proven, even if the derived hypothesis or hypotheses are supported by tests! Why? Let us illustrate this apparent paradox by way of some examples.

First consider the following theory.

Assumption 1: Unicorns eat meat.
Assumption 2: Humans have the same eating patterns as unicorns.
Implication or prediction: Humans eat meat.

You may, as most people would, consider this theory to be absurd, because as far as we know unicorns do not exist. Yet, this theory is not different in form from the theories we considered before. The theory has some concepts or assumptions, as before, that are not directly verifiable. The theory about unicorns leads us to a conclusion that we can test. In fact, we would find evidence that supports the conclusion—in all societies known to anthropology, humans eat meat at least some of the time. Are the assumptions and the implication therefore correct? The answer is no. We cannot ever conclude that the assumptions are correct because the conclusion derivable from them is correct. This is a fundamental principle in logic: a correct conclusion cannot affirm the premises. Indeed, we could substitute other assumptions to arrive at the same conclusion. For example, we could substitute "Loch Ness monsters" for "unicorns" and still derive the prediction that humans eat meat.

We will return below to how we can test a theory even though we can't prove it. But first, let us consider another theory, purely cultural rather than biological, that could also explain a gender difference in aggression.

Theory 3
Assumption 1: Around the world, males and females generally have different role assignments.
Assumption 2: Cross-culturally, males (not females) are generally the warriors.
Assumption 3: Warfare is common around the world.
Assumption 4: Warfare requires aggressive behavior.
Assumption 5: Parents and other caretakers tend to rear children to fit the roles that society expects them to perform.
Assumption 6: Behavior encouraged by parents and caretakers will tend to be common.
Implication or prediction 1: Parents and other caretakers will tend to train boys to be more aggressive than girls.
Implication or prediction 2: Boys will be more aggressive than girls and men will be more aggressive than women.

Notice that Theory 1, Theory 2, and Theory 3 all imply the same prediction— males will be more aggressive than females. The unicorn example shows us intuitively that verification of the conclusion does not affirm the premises. So what does that principle tell us about the three theories? If they all come to the same conclusion, how can we tell which, if any, is correct? We can't tell which is correct. All we can say then is that *the prediction is consistent with a particular theory (or theories).*

As the theory examples show, we can more easily judge a theory if it makes more than one prediction or hypothesis. Even though Theories 1, 2, and 3 imply the same prediction about males being more aggressive than females, Theories 2 and 3 imply additional predictions that can be tested. These additional predictions help us test a theory more precisely, or allow us to compare the applicability of rival theories.

But if we can't prove theories, why bother trying to test them at all? Why not just rely on observations and associations for explanation? This question is easy to answer. As we saw above, the process of stating theory forces us to think about issues that we wouldn't get to if we just stuck with associations. Remember the association we started with—males are more aggressive than females. If we didn't theorize (brainstorm) and test our theories further, our knowledge could not go beyond the simple association. Of course, theorizing itself does not necessarily lead to new understanding. Theories may be incorrect. How can we know they are likely to be incorrect if they are not provable? The position we take on this issue—how to test theory—follows that of Karl Popper (1959)—theories are tested by attempts to **falsify** them. While the conclusions cannot affirm the premises, we are obliged to question the premises if the logical conclusions derived from them are not supported. As Popper has said:

> According to my proposal, what characterizes the empirical method is its manner of exposing to falsification, in every conceivable way, the system to be tested. Its aim is not to save the lives of untenable systems but, on the contrary, to select the one which is by comparison the fittest, by exposing them all to the fiercest struggle for survival. . . . This will be the one which not only has hitherto stood up to the severest tests, but the one which is also testable in the most rigorous way. A theory is a tool which we test by applying it, and which we judge as to its fitness by the results of its applications (1959: 42, 108).

What this means in practical terms is that theories can be evaluated by empirically testing as many of the implications or predictions as possible (sometimes the assumptions can be tested too). Assuming that the tests are well designed, if the predictions or assumptions are not found to be true, the theory is probably not correct. Hence we can reject unsupported theories, that is, theories whose assumptions and predictions have not been supported empirically. Note that a theory that has avoided falsification completely (so far) can be accepted for the time being. But the validity of a theory whose predictions (or assumptions) have not been supported empirically must be questioned. Scientific understanding progresses by the discarding of rival theories that have been tested and falsified.

Before we go to the trouble of trying to test a theory, we should first evaluate it to see if it has the characteristics that could make it scientifically useful. Here are some criteria to evaluate the usefulness of theories:

1. *Theories should be logical.* If the implications or predictions do not follow from the premises, testing the implications cannot test the theory.
2. *Theories should be internally consistent.* Parts should not contradict each other, nor should there be contradictory implications.
3. *At least some of the theoretical concepts must be measurable.* Religious theories, such as the idea that gods are responsible for events, are not testable because there is no empirical way to measure the gods' actions.
4. *There must be at least one derivable proposition (hypothesis) that can be tested and falsified.* It is better if multiple predictions are derivable because that gives the theory more chances to fail or succeed. For example, all three of the theories discussed above share the prediction that males are more aggressive than females. But Theories 2 and 3 have additional testable predictions that may help us evaluate the relative usefulness of the theories.

To sum up, here are some differences between laws (verified hypotheses) and theory (Nagel 1961, chapter 5). Keep in mind that hypotheses (derived predictions) have the same structure as laws. A consistently confirmed hypothesis becomes a law.

- Every concept in a law has a clear way of being measured by some form of observation; theories have at least some concepts or ideas that cannot be measured, at least currently.
- Laws are generalizations from particular instances; a theory may be suggested by data but it cannot be generalized from data. Because a law is based on observations, it may be true even if the theory implying it is false.
- A law (or hypothesis) is formulated in a single statement; theories usually are more complex, consisting of related statements.
- Laws explain a relatively narrow range of things; theories provide explanations for laws and hence generally explain a wider range of phenomena than laws do.

Figure 3.1 identifies the relationships between theory, hypotheses,

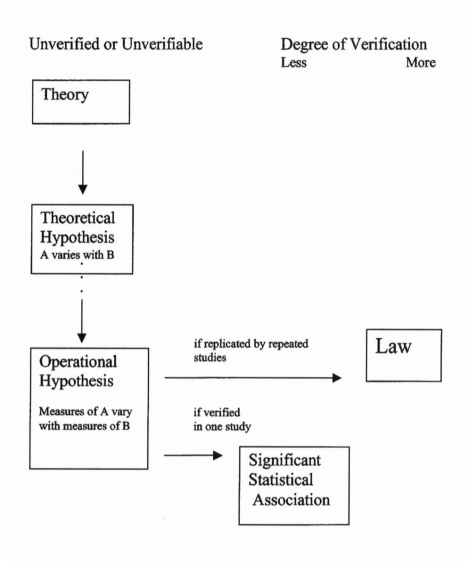

Unverified or Unverifiable   Degree of Verification
                                    Less   More

Theory

Theoretical
Hypothesis
A varies with B

Operational   if replicated by repeated   Law
Hypothesis   studies

Measures of A vary   if verified
with measures of B   in one study

                     Significant
                     Statistical
                      Association

Key:
Down arrow = logical deduction
Down arrow with dots = involves derivation
and imagination (the art of measurement)

Figure 3.1.   Relationships between Theory, Hypotheses, and Laws.

and laws. It is important to add one additional distinction—between a **theoretical hypothesis** and an **operational hypothesis**. The hypothesis that males are more aggressive than females can be tested. But as stated it is still somewhat abstract. We have not explained what we mean by aggressiveness or how we mean to measure it. Without measures, the concept of aggression is still theoretical. It is not until we add operational procedures for measuring concepts (a topic we turn to in the next chapter) that we can say whether the hypothesis is verified or not. This distinction between theoretical and operational hypotheses is important for another reason. It helps remind us that the test of a theory is only as good as the measures and research procedures employed.

NOTES

1. This paragraph is taken from C. R. Ember and M. Ember (1999: 194).

2. For a discussion of some of the research and the findings, see C. R. Ember (1981).

4

The Art of Measurement

The first thing that must be understood about measurement is that nothing is measured directly. This is not just true in the social sciences; it is true also in the physical and biological sciences. To be sure, some measurements are more direct than others. But even our most conventional measures are not so direct. For example, we are so used to a thermometer measuring heat that we may forget that heat is an abstract theoretical concept that refers to the energy generated when molecules are moving. A thermometer reflects the principle that as molecules move more, a substance in a confined space (alcohol, mercury) will expand. We do not see increased heat; we see only the movement of the substance in the confined space (as when the mercury rises in a narrow cylinder). The number we get when we read a thermometer is not the same thing as the "heat" of a substance. And the number read from the thermometer is arbitrary. If we say the temperature is 54, that means nothing by itself. We use the number to see how the "heat" of a substance may change over time, or to compare the "heat" of one substance with the "heat" of another, or to relate "heat" to some other variable. The essential point of a measure (in this case a thermometer) is that it allows us to *compare* (cf. M. Ember 1970: 701).

But if all measurement is indirect, that doesn't mean that all measures are equally good. We are all familiar with inexpensive bathroom scales that give you two different readings if you step on them twice. The trouble with the inexpensive scale is that it is not *reliable*. **Reliability**—consistency or stability—is one of the things we want from a measure. Inexpensive scales are not very *precise* either. That is, it is difficult to measure small fractions of a pound or a kilogram. But even the crudest measures can allow us to discover a pattern (e.g., the range of variation) or a relationship between one thing and another. For example, we don't have a very good way of measuring the height of infants because you have to stretch them out and they don't always cooperate. The ruler we measure them against may be precise, but straightening the baby's limbs is not. It doesn't really matter for most purposes. Medical practitioners can find out a lot about a baby's health and maturation by charting its height (however roughly measured) and weight at each visit and comparing these measures with averages for babies of the same age. Precision is nice, but not always necessary.

The most important requirement of a good measure is that it measures what it purports to measure. If a measure reflects or measures what it is supposed to, we say that it has **validity**. How do we know that a particular measure is valid if it, like all measures, is indirect? Trying to establish validity is one of the hardest things to do and we will discuss it in some detail later.

In order to evaluate a measure it is not just necessary to know the theoretical concept supposedly measured. It is also important to consider the cultural context and the purpose of the study. For example, two researchers might be interested in measuring economic productivity. One researcher might want to measure the average monetary equivalent of goods and services produced by the average adult in a day. But this measure would be meaningless in relatively noncommercial societies because much of production is not for sale; adults mostly produce food and other things for direct use by themselves and their families. A more widely applicable measure of productivity would reflect noncommercial as well as commercial production. Indeed, not all economic output can be measured in monetary terms, even in a society with buying and selling. If you want to measure productivity, even in a commercial society, you have to try to measure the output of all production.

A few more general points about measurement. Be as explicit as possible about what concept you are trying to measure and give others as much information as possible about how you measured that concept. A recipe is an appropriate analogy for the second part—giving others information. If you want a dish to come out the same way each time it is made, you have to try to spell out the ingredients and all the measurement and mixing procedures. (Of course, cookbook writers do not usually spell out their theoretical concepts; but we wouldn't think too much of a recipe that did not operationalize or spell out what you have to do!) Science depends upon replication. If we are to be confident about our findings, other researchers must be able to understand our measures well enough to be able to repeat them. Finally, since all measures are indirect (which is another way of saying that no measure is perfect), it is usually better to measure a concept in multiple ways.

To sum up what we have discussed so far:

- To measure is to compare one thing with another.
- All measures are indirect.
- Measures need to reflect the cultural context and purpose(s) of the study.
- Researchers should strive for reliability, precision, validity, and explicitness.
- Researchers should aim for multiple or alternative measures.

DESIGNING MEASURES FOR CROSS-CULTURAL RESEARCH USING SECONDARY DATA

In chapter 2, we said that the research question suggests much of what the researcher needs to do. Suppose we asked a descriptive question: "What proportion of societies typically have extended families?" We know we have to measure the typical family form in a sample of societies. If we asked a causal question, for example, "Why do some societies typically have extended families?" we would also have to measure the typical family form. However, in contrast to the descriptive question, the causal question hasn't told us what might explain the presence of such families. (The causes or predictors are not specified in the question.) Before we know what else to measure, we need to have at least one idea to test, one hypothesis about why such families exist.

Measures have to be specified for each variable (dependent and independent) in the hypothesis. The first steps involve the following:

1. Theoretically defining the variable of interest (in words or mathematically).
2. Operationally defining the measure(s), which means spelling out in practical terms the steps you need to take to make a decision about where a case falls on the "scale" that you have devised for measuring the variable. This is not always a straightforward process. Designing a measure requires some trial-and-error, and if the scale is too confusing or too hard to apply (because the required information is missing too often), the measure needs to be rethought.

Example: Extended Family Households

To illustrate the processes involved in measurement, let's start with a research question we have investigated (Pasternak, C. R. Ember, and M. Ember, 1976): Why do married couples in some societies typically live with related couples in extended family households, whereas in other societies couples typically live separately (in independent households)? This is a causal question that specifies the dependent variable, in this case, "type of household." By the way the question is phrased, the measure we design requires us to decide how to discover the typical household pattern in a society. The measure should be appropriate for a comparison of societies. Although the concept of extended family household may appear straightforward, we still have to define it explicitly. The researcher should state what an "extended family" means, what a "household" means, and how to decide what is the typical type of household. The researcher may choose to define a family as a social and economic unit consisting minimally of one or more parents and children. An extended family might then be defined as consisting of two or more constituent families connected by a blood tie (most commonly a parent-child or brother-sister tie). And an extended family household might be defined as an extended family that lives co-residentially—in one house or in a compound or group of houses—and functions as an economic unit. An independent family would have only one constituent family. Having defined the concepts, the researcher must then specify the procedure for assessing what type of family is typical in the society. All of these steps are involved in operationalizing the variable of interest.

Definitions are not so hard to arrive at. What requires work is evaluating whether an operational definition is useful or easily applied. This is part of the art of measurement. For example, suppose we decided that in order to assess whether extended families or independent families were typical, we needed information from a census on the actual percentage of households of each type. From a measurement perspective this would be ideal. We could use as our measure the actual percentage of extended family households (0 to 100 percent). This would give us a **ratio measure** (see box 4.1). Other things being equal, a ratio measure (or at least an ordinal measure) is preferable to a nominal measure because we can use more powerful statistical tests with ratio or ordinal measures. (This is because such measures allow us to order our cases according to some scale.) However, pretesting would tell us that very few ethnographers provide the percentage of extended family households or give us the results of censuses. Rather, they usually say things like "extended family households are the norm." Or, "extended families are typical, but younger people are beginning to live in independent households." So our operational definition of percentage of extended family households, although ideal, may not be that useful, if we cannot find enough societies with reports based on household censuses.

What can we do in this predicament? There are three choices:

1. We can stick to our insistence on the best measure and study only those societies for which the ethnography gives us percentages of

Nominal measurement. The simplest form of measurement divides things into discrete sets. The criteria for those sets should be clear and unambiguous so that we can classify a case as belonging to one or another set. If we decide to classify the typical household in a society as extended or independent, we are asking for a nominal classification into two sets. An example of a nominal measure with more than two sets is form of marriage. Anthropologists typically classify marriages as monogamous, polygynous (one husband with two or more wives), or polyandrous (one wife with two or more husbands). While numbers may be assigned to these sets for entry into a computer, the numbers only convey that the cases are different.

While nominal scales are often referred to as the simplest form of measurement, they sometimes are the highest that can be meaningfully used. Take the concept of gender. If a society recognizes two genders of male and female, most researchers will simply want to classify people as one gender or the other.

Ordinal measurement. An ordinal measure adds a modifier of "more" or "less" to the concept of difference. If we line up individuals by their relative size we can give them rank order numbers that convey more or less height. If we give two people the same number, we convey that they are not different. Ordinal categories can be many, as in the lineup of the height of individuals, or they can be few such as "frequent," "occasional," and "rare." While numbers may be assigned to these relative positions, the numbers convey difference and order only.

Interval measurement and ratio measurement. If we wanted a measure of height we wouldn't normally line people up in rank order unless we had not come equipped with a good long ruler. A good ruler has equally spaced intervals on a standardized metric. Instead of saying that one person is taller than another, we can say that they are taller by a certain number of centimeters or inches. With two numbers to compare on an interval or ratio scale, we can legitimately describe the *amount of difference* when we compare cases. From a statistical perspective, interval and ratio measures are essentially treated the same. Mathematically, however, a ratio scale has one additional property compared with an interval scale—it has a "true zero point." A thermometer calibrated on the Fahrenheit or Celsius scale is an interval scale, not a ratio scale, because the zero-point on both these scales does not mean the absence of heat. The Kelvin scale, on the other hand, is a ratio scale because "0" means that there is no motion of molecules and no "heat." An absolute zero point allows us to multiply and divide the numbers on the scale meaningfully. We can describe a person who is 6 feet high as twice as tall as a person who is 3 feet tall because the zero point on a ruler means "0" length. But we cannot say that when it is 60° Fahrenheit it is twice as hot as when it is 30° Fahrenheit.

Box 4.1. Types of Measurement

Examples of interval and ratio scales:

population density
average rainfall in a year
population of the largest community
number of people in a polity
annual income
number of people in a household

Transforming one scale into another: All other things being equal, it is preferable to use a "higher" level of measurement. That is, an interval or ratio scale is preferable to an ordinal scale. An ordinal scale is preferable to a nominal scale. Leaving aside the concepts that are not meaningfully transformable, we can often imagine how we could transform a scale. As we saw in the extended family example, we can have a nominal scale that contrasts extended family household societies with independent family households. If we prefer, we can change the variable into an ordinal scale by relabeling the variable "frequency of extended family households" and we could classify societies as having frequencies that are "very high," "moderately high," "moderately low," or "infrequent or rare," according to the scale described on page 43. If we had enough information, we could employ a ratio scale with "percentage of households that are extended family households." The researcher must be careful not to invoke a higher order of measurement or more precision when the data do not warrant it.

Box 4.1.   Continued

  each type of household (or percentages can be calculated from the quantitative information provided); we may have to expand our search (enlarge our sample) to find enough cases that have such precise information.
2. We can choose not to do the study because we can't measure the concept exactly how we want to.
3. We can redesign our measure to incorporate descriptions in words that are not based on census materials.

Faced with these three choices, most cross-cultural researchers would opt to redesign the measure to incorporate word descriptions. (That would be our choice.) Word descriptions do convey information about degree, even if not as precisely as percentages. If an ethnographer says "extended family households are typical," we do not know if that means 50 percent or 100 percent, but we can be very confident it does not mean 0 to 40 percent. And we can be fairly sure it does not mean 40 to 49 percent. If the relative frequency of extended family households (measured on the basis of words) is related to something else, we should be able to see the relationship even though we are not able to use a percentage measure based on numerical information. Relative frequency is a type of **ordinal measure,** where numbers on the scale convey an ordering from more to less. A measure of relative frequency of extended family households might read something like what follows.

Code extended family household as:

4. *Very high* in frequency if the ethnographer describes this type of household as the norm or typical in the absence of any indication of another common type of household. Phrases like "almost all households are extended" are clear indicators. *Do not use discussions of the "ideal" household to measure relative frequency, unless there are indications that the ideal is also practiced. If there is a developmental cycle, such as the household splitting up when the third generation reaches a certain age, do not use this category. Rather, you should use scale score 3 if the extended family household remains together for a substantial portion of the life cycle or scale score 2 if the household remains together only briefly.*

3. *Moderately high* in frequency if the ethnographer describes another fairly frequent household pattern but indicates that extended family households are still the most common.

2. *Moderately low* in frequency if the ethnographer describes extended family households as alternative or a second choice (another form of household is said to be typical).

1. *Infrequent or rare* if another form of household is the only form of household mentioned and if the extended family form is mentioned as absent or an unusual situation. *Do not infer the absence of extended families merely from the absence of discussion of family and household type. To use this category, the ethnographer must explicitly discuss family and household.*

Don't know if there is no information on form of household, or there is contradictory information. (We usually use discontinuous numbers like 8 for no information and 9 for contradictory information; these numbers need to be dropped before performing statistical tests. The discontinuity helps remind the researcher that these numbers should not be included.)

It is very important to tell your coders how to infer that something is rare or absent. Most ethnographers do not give an inventory of what is missing in a society. Researchers therefore have to specify the appropriate rules for inferring rarity or absence. In scale point 1 above, our rules specify that the coder is not allowed to say extended families are absent in the absence of information. If there is no information the coder must say "don't know." We will return to this issue later.

A final part of the instructions is to specify how to find the information required to make a decision. Many cross-cultural researchers use the Human Relations Area Files (HRAF) Collection of Ethnography (see the description in chapter 6 and the appendix on how to use the HRAF Collection). This full-text database is complexly indexed by subject matter, so that a researcher can rapidly find paragraphs relevant to the indexed subject. (Word searches are also possible in the electronic HRAF, or you could search using a combination of index categories and words in texts). It is very easy to find the relevant information when the subject matter of interest to the research is clearly indexed in the HRAF files. In regard to our concern here, the HRAF Collection of Ethnography has one subject category (592, Household) that can be consulted. Another advantage of this database is that the independent and dependent variables can be measured in separate steps, which minimizes the chance that knowing one variable will influence the coding of another variable.

Notice the italicized caveats in the above scale on extended family households. These caveats are usually inserted after the researcher realizes the practical problems that may arise when looking at actual ethnographies (this stage is what we call *pretesting*). Additional *pretesting* should be done using coders who have not had anything to do with creating the scale. It may turn out that four distinctions are too difficult to apply to the word descriptions usually found in ethnographies, so a researcher might want to collapse the scale a little. Or, it may turn out that two coders do not frequently agree with each other. If so, the investigator may have to spell out the rules a little more. And if we use the *ordinal* scale described above, what do we do when the ethnography actually gives us precise numbers or percentages for a case? It is usually easy to fit those numbers into the word scale (or to average two adjacent scale scores). So, for instance, if 70 percent of the households have extended families, and 30 percent are independent, we would choose scale score 3. But we might decide to use two scales: a more precise one based on numerical measurement (percentages) for those cases with numbers or percentages, the other scale relying on words (when the ethnography provides only words). C. R. Ember et al. (1991) recommend the use of both types of scale when possible. The advantage of using two scales of varying precision is that the more precise one (the quantitative scale) should be more strongly related to other variables than the less precise scale. (The less precise scale should be less accurate than the more precise scale, assuming that the less precise one has to rely sometimes on ambiguous words.) Stronger results with the more precise scale would increase our confidence that the relationship observed even with the less precise scale is true.

Alternative to New Measures: Using Existing Measures

The measurement scale described above is a hypothetical one. In our study of extended family households (Pasternak, C. R. Ember, and M. Ember 1976) we actually decided to use an existing measure of extended family households that was used in the *Ethnographic Atlas* (Murdock 1967) for our dependent variable. We had a lot of discussion about the wisdom of this choice. Our main reason for deciding to use an existing measure was that we knew we had to code the independent variable ourselves. As far as we were aware, "incompatible activity requirements," our independent variable, had never been measured before. (Incompatible activity requirements refers to the need for a given gender to do two different tasks at the same time in different places, such as agricultural work and childtending; we reasoned that with such requirements, two or more individuals of the same gender would be needed in the household—hence extended family households would be favored.) We thought it wiser not to code both the independent and dependent variables ourselves. After all, it was our theory we were testing. One of the maxims in science is to try to minimize unconscious biasing of the results. So we decided to measure incompatibility requirements ourselves and to create a score on extended family households using ratings from the *Ethnographic Atlas* (Murdock 1967: column 14) on extended family households. An additional advantage to using Murdock's measure is time. If we coded both the independent and dependent variables ourselves, it would have taken us a lot longer to measure our variables.

The drawback to using a previous researcher's measure is that it may be difficult to be confident that the previous measure is actually measuring what you want to be measuring. *The most serious mistake is to use an existing measure that is not really what you want conceptually.* As we discuss below, lack of fit between the theoretical concept and the operational measure is a serious source of error. In our case, we could be fairly confident about Murdock's measure of type of household. From what we had read of his writings on social structure, his definitions of family and household were similar to ours. (He was Melvin Ember's mentor in graduate school at Yale.)

If you do decide to use someone else's measure, your operational measure becomes a description of how you used the other researcher's scale. If the other researcher's definitions are published in an accessible place, you can refer the reader to them without repeating all the definitions. For instance, we were able to say the following:

Extended family households were considered to be present if the *Atlas* said the case typically had extended family households (E, F, or G in Column 14) and were considered to be absent if the *Atlas* said the case typically had independent families (M, N, O, P, Q, R, or S in Column 14). By extended family household, the *Atlas* means that at least two related families, disregarding polygamous unions, comprise the household—which is equivalent to our concern in this study (Pasternak, C. R. Ember, and M. Ember 1976: 119).

As it happened, incompatible activity requirements (as measured by us) strongly predicted extended family households (as measured by Murdock [1967]). But what if the results hadn't worked out so well? We might then have concluded that our theory was questionable. But it is also possible to get falsifying results if you have too much measurement error. At that point, we might have decided to measure extended family households on our own, using a new ordinal scale, to see if the results would improve.

MINIMIZING ERROR IN THE DESIGN OF MEASURES IN SECONDARY COMPARISONS

Measures are designed to tap theoretical concepts. Ideally we want the measure of a concept to be free of error. If a measure taps the concept exactly, it would be a valid measure. The more the measured score departs from the theoretical construct, the less valid is the measure. In secondary comparisons, error can come from a variety of sources. There may be errors by the ethnographer or the original informants, and there may be errors by those reading and coding the ethnographic information for measures. These types of errors and the steps that can be taken to minimize them will be addressed in the next chapter. Here we address the errors that may result from the lack of fit between the theoretical concept and the designed measure. If the designed measure is measuring something other than the theoretical construct, the researcher is building in serious error, which no amount of carefulness in other aspects of the research design can undo. For the whole point of deriving a hypothesis from a theory is to test that theory. If the measures of the concepts in the theory are far removed from the constructs—if the measures are not valid—it is not legitimate to claim that the tests using those measures can allow us to evaluate the theory.

Types of Validity Used in Secondary Cross-Cultural Research

How can validity be established? The dilemma of all research is that theoretical constructs cannot be measured directly. Therefore there is never any certainty that a measure measures what it is supposed to measure. Even though all measurement is indirect and therefore validity cannot ever be established beyond all doubt (Campbell 1988), some measures are more direct and are therefore more likely to be valid than others. So, for example, more direct measures arouse little doubt that they are measuring what they are supposed to measure. They have high **face validity**; there is little or no need to justify why we are confident about their validity. Other things being equal, we suggest that cross-culturalists try to use measures that are as direct as possible, because less inference and less guesswork generally yields more accuracy and hence stronger results (assuming that you are dealing with a true relationship). For example, when a cross-culturalist wants to measure whether a husband and wife work together, it is more direct to use a measure that is based on explicit ethnographers' reports of work patterns than to infer the work pattern from general statements about how husbands and wives get along (C. R. Ember et al. 1991: 193). A measure based on how well husbands and wives get along would have low face validity as a measure of husbands and wives working together, but a measure based on ethnographer reports of work patterns would have high face validity.

Let's consider the hypothetical measure we constructed (described above) for the frequency of extended family households. The measure we ourselves designed would require the coder to read ethnographers' statements about family type and use the ethnographers' words about frequency to judge the prevalence of extended family households. The measure is very close in meaning to the theoretical construct and on the face of it seems valid.

While direct measures with high face validity are preferable, sometimes a researcher wants to measure something more difficult. The theoretical construct may be quite abstract. Consider the following constructs: community integration, emotional expressiveness, the status of women, or cultural complexity. It is hard to imagine a clear, direct measure of any of these constructs. Rather, we might imagine a lot of different indicators. For example, with respect to the status of women, we may imagine that it could be reflected in leadership positions, in decision-making in the household, in the gender and power of the gods, and so on. Similarly, cultural complexity may be indicated by subsistence technology, the number of different specialists, the degree to which there is a hierarchy of political authorities, and so on.

Other types of validation techniques are harder to use in cross-cultural research using secondary data, but they may be useful in comparisons of field data. These validation techniques involve showing that the new measure is highly correlated with another generally accepted measure (the criterion). The criterion variable may pertain to the future (such as future school performance), the past (prior school performance), or it may be another measure pertaining to roughly the same time.

When no clearly accepted measure is available as the criterion, a measure may be judged in terms of **content validity**—the degree to which "a specified domain of content is sampled" (Nunnally 1978: 91). If ability in some subject is to be measured, a test that covers a lot of different domains would probably be more valid than a test covering only a few selected domains. In cross-cultural studies of abstract constructs, it may be a good idea as you begin to develop your measures to measure items across a wide variety of domains. So, for example, in order to assess the status of women (an abstract construct), Whyte (1978) measured fifty-two different variables that might tap the relative status of women in a wide array of domains. Some of those domains were family life and decision-making, economic roles and control of resources, political leadership, and religious beliefs and practices. Broude and Greene (1983), looking at husband-wife intimacy, measured patterns of eating, sleeping, leisure-time activities, work relations, and husbands' attendance at the birth of a child. Perhaps the most widespread use of content validity is with regard to measures of cultural complexity. For example, Carneiro (Carneiro and Tobias 1963 and Carneiro 1970) measured as many as 618 traits covering a broad range of domains presumably relating to complexity. Other measures of cultural complexity use fewer traits, but most span a broad array of domains. The presumption behind the concept of *content validity* is that a measure is more likely to be valid if it taps into all or most of the relevant domains.

Does this mean that the more traits (or items) included, the better the measure? Not necessarily. First, items that do not tap the same dimension of variation do not improve a measure. It is possible to discover whether items belong together in a given scale (see Weller 1998, and Handwerker and Borgatti 1998, for an introduction to the voluminous literature on methods of scaling). Second, there are practical issues to consider as well as theoretical ones. Too many items can make the research impractical. In conducting a personal interview, too many questions can lead to fatigue (on the part of the researcher as well as the interviewee). In cross-cultural research using ethnographic materials, measuring even a simple trait could take thirty to sixty minutes of reading per case, in our experience. So measuring hundreds of traits would be a formidable task and might lead one to sacrifice other principles of good research design, such as the desirability of studying a random sample of cases that was large enough to allow for statistically significant results even with a lot of missing data.

Statistical techniques can be used to test whether a set of items belongs together. Such tests can be done on small samples to pare down the list of items that need to be used on larger samples. In scaling items or traits that may or may not belong together, there are some general principles.

First, if all the traits or items employed tap the same underlying concept (dimension), they should all be associated with each other, at least to a moderate degree. If you have several measures of baby care—dealing separately with how much the mother holds, feeds, and plays with a baby—they may correlate with each other. But they may not. The researcher may find that various traits have a more complicated or multidimensional structure. For example, in many societies a sibling carries the infant around most of the time, and brings the baby to the mother only for nursing. Thus, it may turn out that not all aspects of baby care cluster together along one dimension of more or less attentiveness. It may be necessary to use two or more scales to tap the multiple dimensions of baby care. Second, if all the traits or items are not indicators of the same construct, it is nearly always possible to discover how many dimensions account for their similarities and differences (Weller 1998; Handwerker and Borgatti 1998).

In the case of cultural complexity, we have scales that use many or only a few traits, from more than 600 (Carneiro 1970: 854–70) to three (Naroll 1956) to two (Marsh 1967). Researchers developing new scales try to compare them with previously developed scales. As it turns out, all of these scales are highly correlated with each other (Peregrine, Ember, and Ember 2000). The concept of **convergent validity** (Campbell and Fiske 1959) refers to the situation of strong intercorrelations among a number of independent measures. If a number of different scales are strongly related, researchers could decide to use the scale or scales that are easier to apply or that best fit the theoretical purposes of their research.

Suppose a researcher is interested in general trends in cultural evolution. In this case, it makes the most sense to use a measure that is designed to tap a sequence of development. For example, one could try to use a **Guttman scale**. This kind of scale is hierarchical. The items are listed in an evolutionary order. If a case has the highest item on the scale, it is likely to have all the other items. If it has a score halfway down, it is likely to have half the items. This steplike feature holds for scores anywhere on the scale. Each case is scored as having either the trait present (in which case it receives a 1 for that trait) or the trait absent (in which case it receives a 0 for that trait). Linton Freeman (1957; as described in Tatje and Naroll 1970) found that the following items scaled in the hierarchical order shown below:

1. Presence or absence of trade with other societies.
2. Presence or absence of a subsistence economy based primarily on agriculture or pastoralism.

3. Presence or absence of social stratification or slavery.
4. Presence or absence of full-time governmental specialists.
5. Presence or absence of full-time religious or magical specialists.
6. Presence or absence of secondary tools (tools fashioned exclusively for the manufacture of other tools).
7. Presence or absence of full-time craft specialists.
8. Presence or absence of a standard medium of exchange with a value fixed at some worth other than its commodity value.
9. Presence or absence of a state of at least 10,000 in population.
10. Presence or absence of towns exceeding 1,000 in population.
11. Presence or absence of a complex, unambiguously written language.

If a case receives a score of 11 on this scale, it means two things. One is that it has a complex, written language. The second thing implied by a score of 11 is that the case is likely to have all the other items. That is, each score implies the presence also of the traits marked by lower numbers. Notice that the scale is hierarchical only in one direction; the presence of a town of more than 1,000 population (a score of 10) does not imply a written language (a score of 11), but it does imply the presence of item 9 (a state of at least 10,000 population). Note too that the other traits lower in the scale may not be present with certainty, but if the scale is a Guttman-type scale, it is very likely that the traits lower are present. Most cases with a scale score of 6, for example, would also have items 1 through 5.

COMPARATIVE PROJECTS COLLECTING PRIMARY DATA

Since this book focuses primarily on secondary cross-cultural comparisons (using other people's data), we will only briefly discuss measurement in the field. Other methods sources should be consulted for detailed discussions on collecting primary data in the field and judging informant accuracy (see, for example, Romney et al. 1986; Bernard 1994; Johnson and Sackett 1998; Weller 1998). And see the Munroes (1991a, 1991b) and Johnson (1991) for extended discussions of comparative field studies. Some measurement techniques lend themselves more readily to comparison than others. While participant observation and unstructured interviewing are usually a necessary first step in any field study, such techniques are less likely to lead to comparable data-gathering and measurement across sites than more structured interviews and systematic observation. It goes without saying that any measure used across sites needs to be applicable to all the sites. Most comparative field studies deal with general domains of life that are found in all societies—for example, words and classification of colors, kin, animals, and plants, ideas about illness, raising children, and social behaviors.

Comparing Primary Data from Field Studies: Behavior Observations

A comparative researcher may be interested in kinds of data that are very unlikely to be described in the ethnographic record. So conventional cross-cultural comparison, using the secondary data in the ethnographic record, is not possible. If you can't find enough information in ethnographies to measure the variables of interest to you, what else can you do? One possibility is to do a comparative field study (R. L. Munroe and R. H. Munroe 1991a, 1991b). If there is little relevant ethnography available, you could collect behavior observations systematically in more than one field site on the variables of interest.

But, as Beatrice and John Whiting (1970: 284) pointed out, systematic behavior observation is so time-consuming that comparative field workers should only consider it if the interviewing of informants cannot provide valid data on the domain in question. For example, adults (particularly males) may not be able to report accurately on child rearing or child behavior. Or ethnographers (generally males, in the early years of anthropology) may not have been interested generally in collecting such information. Either way, there were few extensive descriptions of child rearing in the ethnographic record as of the 1950s. Therefore, child behavior and child rearing were domains that the Whitings thought needed to be observed firsthand. The Six Cultures project (J. W. M. Whiting et al. 1966; B. B. Whiting and J. W. M. Whiting 1975) and the Four Cultures Project directed by Robert L. and Ruth H. Munroe (R. L. Munroe et al. 2000; see references therein) are examples of comparative field projects that measured children's behavior. To illustrate how you can design measures for comparative field studies, we focus here on how children's aggressive behavior was measured by the Munroes (R. L. Munroe et al. 2000).

As with all scientific measures, it is necessary to spell out as much of the procedures as possible. The investigators (R. L. Munroe et al. 2000: 7) tell us that they coded behavior observations following the classification suggested by the Whitings (B. B. Whiting and J. W. M. Whiting 1975: 54–65). The Whitings classified social behaviors into twelve major categories. The Munroes considered three of them to involve "aggressive behavior" (R. L. Munroe et al. 2000: 7)—assault, horseplay, and symbolic aggression. The Whitings (1975: 57–62) suggested that the observer consider whether the observed acts of physical aggression were serious or playful. Serious assaults included such behaviors as striking, slapping, or kicking someone else; playful or sociable assaults consisted of behaviors such as friendly wrestling or backslapping. Symbolic aggression included threats or insults by word or gesture as well as attempts to frighten or derogate another person. Responsible aggression—for example, aggression that was legitimately administered as a punishment—was excluded by the Whitings from the aggressive categories.

The Munroes (R. L. Munroe et al. 2000) trained local native assistants to observe the social behavior of children and record the behavior according to the twelve major behavior categories specified by the Whitings. The Munroes planned to construct a proportion score for each type of aggression observed (the number of each type of aggression divided by the total number of social acts observed). Each observer was assigned children to observe; on a given day, the observer would look for a particular (focal) child in his or her natural setting. If the focal child was interacting with at least two other persons, the observer was told to watch for any social behavior on the part of the focal child (either the child initiating a social interaction with someone else or the child responding to someone else). The first observed social behavior was described. The descriptive protocol included the details of the behavior, the type of behavior that the child or another individual may have initiated (which of the twelve categories the behavior belonged to), the type of response to the initiation, and the individuals within close proximity to the focal child. In contrast to the Whitings' Six Cultures project, in which the observers recorded behaviors for five minutes, the Munroes decided to record only the first social behavior observed. With the measures they constructed, the Munroes demonstrated significant overall differences by gender—male children were generally more aggressive, in all categories of aggression but especially in assault. In addition, aggression generally declines with age and is much more likely the more male peers are present in the social setting. The Munroes' findings from the four field sites are generally consistent with previous research in other cultures employing somewhat different measurement techniques. For example, the Six Cultures project (J. W. M. Whiting et al. 1966; B. B. Whiting and J. W. M. Whiting 1975) used longer behavior protocols (five minutes in length). Robert Munroe (personal communication) suggests that the short observations the Munroes employed (in which the observer only records the first social behavior seen) are less intrusive and allow the collection of observations over a larger span of time. The disadvantage is that the observer is not catching sequences of behaviors.

The major obstacle to choosing to use systematic behavior observations in comparative field studies is that they take a long time to do (you have to spend considerable time in the field, in more than one place) and they are very expensive (not only must the investigators be supported, but also the native observers). So, as much as most researchers would like to obtain data directly, by comparative field studies, conventional cross-cultural research using the data already in the ethnographic record is much more feasible. But remember: you can't do a conventional type of study if you can't think of how you can use data in the ethnographic record to measure the variables of interest to you.

5

Minimizing Error

In the last chapter, we discussed the validity of measures, that is, how a measure is invalid if it does not measure what it purports to measure. If the way the measure is designed does not tap the theoretical construct it is supposed to tap, there is no possible remedy short of redesigning the measure. The measurement process could entail other kinds of error too, which we deal with in this chapter. We discuss strategies for minimizing the possible effects of these other kinds of error, which may be **systematic** (biased in some fashion, usually in one direction) or **random** (in any direction). These errors can come from ethnographers, informants, coders, or coding rules. Ethnographers may not mention something or they may underreport it (e.g., not mention the number of Western objects in the village). Or they may overreport (e.g., overemphasize the unilineality of the descent system to fit reality into an ideal type). Informants may underreport (e.g., not mention an illegal or disapproved activity) or overreport an activity they believe will make them look better in the eyes of the ethnographer. Coders may interpret ethnography from the point of view of their own culture, their gender, or their personality. Finally, the coding rules may not be specific enough, which can increase error. We can try to minimize all of these kinds of error in the way we design a study.

In terms of their effects on relationships between variables, systematic error is not serious if it occurs consistently and mostly in one variable. This is because one variable still predicts the other in a known way. Figures 5.1a and 5.1b illustrate this situation. Figure 5.1a shows a relationship between variables X and Y. X predicts Y in a perfectly linear way; as X increases by one point, Y increases by one point. In figure

5.1b, the relationship is computed again, except this time X is inflated by one point. When X should be 1, it is 2. When X should be 2, it is 3. This is a systematic error in one direction. Notice, however, that the relationship is still perfect. We can predict Y precisely by knowing X. This is not to say that it doesn't matter if X is systematically distorted. For some research purposes, it would matter. If we wanted to describe the average value of X in a sample, the average would not be correct if it were systematically inflated. In figure 5.1a, the average X score is 3. In figure 5.1b, the average X score is 4. If we wanted a formula for the line that best describes the relationship between X and Y, it would be different in the two figures. For the first figure the line would be $Y = X$; for the second figure it would be $Y = X - 1$. However, most researchers examine relationships between variables. For this purpose, consistent systematic error in one variable would not matter at all. Variables X and Y would still be perfectly related in a linear fashion.

What if there were systematic error in both variables? Would this change things in any appreciable way? The answer is generally no if the errors are *not correlated* (the errors on one variable do not predict errors on the other variable). Consider the situation where there is a perfect relationship between X and Y. Systematic error in both variables will not change the relationship if the systematic error occurs in all cases. Imagine that both variables X and Y are always inflated by one point. In this case the relationship would look like figure 5.1a again, except that there would be no cases of $X = 1$ and no cases of $Y = 1$. When X is 2, Y would be 2; when X is 3, Y would be 3. If there is really a perfect relationship between X and Y, but there is systematic error in some but not all of the cases, the relationship will only be a little weaker. Imagine that of the five cases shown in figure 5.1b, one of the cases does not have a systematic error (i.e., the case that is 5 on X and 4 on Y). The graph would look like that shown in figure 5.1c. The case at 4 and 4 (which was at 5, 4 in figure 5.1b) is now at its true scale score. Notice that the relationship is no longer perfect because it is not possible to draw a straight line between all the points. (The line shown is a line that the computer program draws to try to get the best fit; we will discuss this more fully in chapter 8.) Instead of a perfect relationship, with a perfect correlation of 1.00, the computer now calculates a correlation of .959. Ironically, *no* systematic error and 100 percent systematic error have the same effects—they do not change a relationship at all.

Let us now consider a hypothetical nonrelationship between variables X and Y (see table 5.1a). One variable is not predictable from the other: Y is equally likely to be present or absent when X is present and vice versa. Now imagine another table with both variables subject to systematic inflation; that is, some proportion of "Absent Xs" and some proportion of "Absent Ys" are falsely classified as present. Since Variable X is absent in

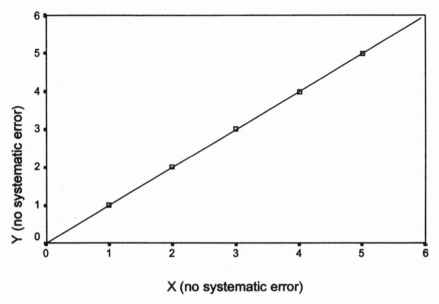

Figure 5.1a.   Perfect Relationship between X and Y (no systematic error).

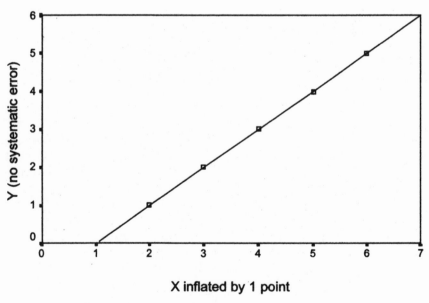

Figure 5.1b.   Relationship between X and Y (X inflated by one point).

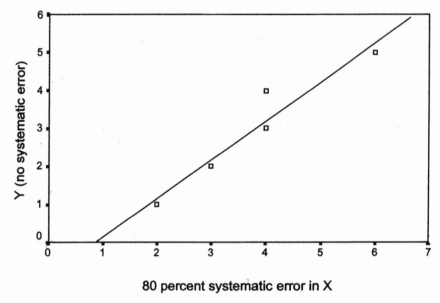

80 percent systematic error in X

Figure 5.1c.   Relationship between X and Y (80% systematic error in X).

the top row and Variable Y is absent in the left column, some cases will
move down from the upper row to the bottom row, some cases will move
from the left column to the right column, and some cases will move diag-
onally from the upper left cell to the lower right if both X and Y are inflated. The lower right cell will always pick up cases and the upper left
cell will always lose cases. Table 5.1b shows the expected effect of 20 percent systematic error in both variables X and Y when the errors are *not correlated*. (This means that X is not more likely to be inflated if Y is, and vice
versa.) If there are fifty cases of X absent, to have 20 percent error overall
means that twenty of fifty cases or 40 percent of the absent cases must be
misclassified from absent to present. Our simulation shows that systematic error in two variables with uncorrelated errors would not create a
relationship when there is none. Not only is the result in table 5.1b not
statistically significant (see chapter 8 for a discussion of statistical significance), but knowing the value of X does not help us predict the value of
Y at all. This can best be illustrated by showing the percentage of the row
in each cell. As table 5.1c shows, the cells in the top and the bottom rows
of the table have the same percentages. This means that knowing the
value of variable X does not improve our ability to predict Y. So even
though we have many more "present" cases because of systematic inflation, we would not be led to a faulty conclusion about an association between X and Y.

Table 5.1a.   Expected Relationship between Variable X and Variable Y with No Underlying Association

		Variable Y		
		Absent	*Present*	*Total*
Variable	Absent	25	25	50
X	Present	25	25	50
	Total	50	50	100

Table 5.1b.   Expected Relationship between Variable X (20% inflation) and Variable Y (20% inflation) with No Underlying Association

		Variable Y (20% inflation)		
		Absent	*Present*	*Total*
Variable	Absent	9	21	30
X (20%	Present	21	49	70
inflation)	Total	30	70	100

Table 5.1c.   Showing Table 5.1b with Low Percentages

			Variable Y (20% inflation)		
			Absent	*Present*	*Total*
Variable X	Absent	Count	9	21	30
(20%		% within Variable			
inflation)		X (20% inflation)	30.0%	70.0%	100.0%
	Present	Count	21	49	70
		% within Variable			
		X (20% inflation)	30.0%	70.0%	100.0%
	Total	Count	30	70	100
		% within Variable			
		X (20% inflation)	30.0%	70.0%	100.0%

As Naroll (1962, 1970b) noted, systematic error in two variables (double systematic error) could conceivably create a relationship when there really is none. We think Naroll must have been thinking of the situation where the systematic errors *are correlated*, that is, the pattern of errors on one variable influences the pattern of errors on the other variable. This could conceivably happen if ethnographers or coders believe that two features should co-occur. If they believe that if X is present Y should be present too, they might inflate one variable falsely if the other is present. Table 5.2a diagrams this situation. As indicated in the fourth column, the errors occur only when one variable is absent and the other is present. If the error is always inflationary, such cases will falsely move to the present/present cell as the "error" column and the "move to" column show in table 5.2a. In this particular scenario, we assume an overall error rate of 10 percent (ten of 100) in variable X and 10 percent error (ten of 100) in variable Y.

However, all the errors (ten in variable X and ten in variable Y) have to occur within the fifty cases that are absent on one variable and present on the other. This means that twenty of the fifty such cases, 40 percent of those cases, have to be distorted. How likely is this to happen? We think rarely or never. This is an almost unimaginable amount of error. It is one thing to inflate a score on a five-point scale by one point, but it is highly unlikely that ethnographers or coders could imagine so often that something is present when it is really absent. We have simulated this situation and have found that double systematic error of 10 percent, if the errors are correlated (occur in the same cases), would produce a falsely significant result with a modest correlation of .375 (see table 5.2b).

In all other circumstances (where the errors are not correlated), double systematic error will be unlikely to produce a significant result if there is no relationship in the first place.

Table 5.2a. Double Systematic Error (10% Inflation on Each Variable) with the Errors Correlated

Original Values X	Y	number	errors	move to	Resultant
absent	absent	25	0		25
absent	present	25	10 inflated Xs	present/present	15
present	absent	25	10 inflated Ys	present/present	15
present	present	25	0	+20	45

Table 5.2b. Expected Relationship between Variable X (with 10% correlated error) and Variable Y (with 10% correlated error). The type of correlated error is shown in Table 5.2a

		Variable Y (with 10% correlated error)		
		Absent	Present	Total
Variable	Absent	25	15	40
X (with 10%	Present	15	45	60
correlated)	Total	40	60	100
error)				

In contrast to systematic error, which may (albeit rarely) produce statistically significant results that are in fact false, **random error**, which is error in any direction, consistently detracts from the researcher's ability to find significant relationships (Blalock 1972: 414). The nice thing about random error, if one can say such a thing, is that it is free from bias. If a mistake is made, it is likely to be wrong up *or* down on the measurement scale. Thus, random errors tend to cancel each other out. Imagine that you are trying to measure the length of a baby who doesn't like being measured. The baby may curl up or stretch out, so its length will sometimes be inflated and sometimes deflated. Repeated measurements will likely average out to the real value, but the more random error in a particular measurement, the less likely you will see a significant relationship with another measure.

There is no question that random error will make true relationships look weaker. Consider the perfect linear relationship shown in figure 5.1a. While systematic error in every case could conceivably preserve the perfect relationship, but only if the departure was unidirectional and consistent, random errors would mostly pull the case off the "true" line. If there is no true relationship, random errors will move the cases in all directions, and there will still be no relationship. For example, some cases from the upper left box or cell (in a 4-celled table) will move right, some in the bottom right will move left. This kind of thing will happen in every cell, so we are likely to end up with more or less the same numbers in every cell. Random errors are not likely to create a relationship when there is none.

WAYS TO MINIMIZE ERROR IN RESEARCH DESIGN

Obviously it would be best not to have any error at all. As we have seen above, except for double systematic errors that are correlated, systematic and random errors generally make it harder to see a true relationship because the observed correlation is usually weakened. How much you worry about error generally depends on two things: whether you are looking for robust versus weak relationships; and whether you are more concerned about accepting a relationship that is really false than rejecting a relationship that is really true. If you are interested mostly in robust relationships, a small amount of error should not reduce your chances of finding such relationships. Actually, when you find a significant result, your confidence in the result should be enhanced, considering that random error in the measures has probably weakened the observed relationship. Almost all types of error detract from a relationship, so it is very unlikely that error would completely obscure a robust finding. The worst that might happen is that error made the finding less robust. However, if you are interested in relationships that might be small in nature, error of any kind is serious and will probably reduce your chances of finding any relationship.

Some ways of dealing with error are more time-consuming than others. The most efficient way to minimize error is to head it off in your design. Here are some simple tips, which we spell out below.

- Try to measure variables in ways that require the least inference on the part of coders (see the section below on high versus low inference variables). More inference leaves room for systematic as well as random errors.
- Pretest your measures on some cases that are not part of the study. If you yourself cannot get strong results, it is unlikely that anyone else will be able to. After you think that the instructions and codes are clear, get some other people to use the instructions to code a few cases. Discuss any disagreements in the codings. Often such discussion will make you aware of difficulties or obscurities in the coding rules. If inferences are required, give instructions about appropriate and inappropriate ways to make inferences.
- Adhere to a time and place focus (per case) for coding your variables. The variables in each case should be coded for the same place and time (unless you are deliberately looking to measure a lagged effect). This should minimize the possibility of random error reducing your observed correlations.

High- Versus Low-Inference Variables

No matter how direct a measure may seem conceptually, it may require a high degree of inference by the coder if there is little relevant information in ethnographies. The terms "high-inference" and "low-inference" variables, first introduced by John W. M. Whiting (1981), provide a useful scheme for thinking about how to design measures. Variables that require low inference on the part of the coder deal with visible traits or customs, usually reported by ethnographers, and easily located in ethnographies (Bradley 1987, 1989; Burton and White 1987; J. W. M. Whiting 1981; cf. White 1990). High-inference variables require complex coding judgments and are therefore difficult to code reliably. The codings of low-inference variables are less likely to contain error, and independent coders are therefore more likely to agree on codings. For example, Bradley (1987) compared her codings of presence versus absence of the plow with Pryor's (1985) codings for twenty-three societies; there was 96 percent agreement between the two data sets. The only disagreement was about a case that Pryor himself expressed uncertainty about. Thus, presence or absence of the plow, which ethnographers can observe and record without interpretation, is a low-inference variable. Other low-inference variables include the type of carrying device for infants (if any), shapes of houses, domestic animals, and major crops, and many elements of material culture (Bradley 1987; Burton and White 1987; and J. W. M. Whiting 1981).

Note that the dimension of low versus high inference may be uncorrelated with the dimension of more versus less direct measurement. Presence or absence of the plow may be measurable with low inference but if you consider it to be a proxy measure for the judgement that men do most of the agricultural work, then your measure would be low inference but indirect.

Because the measurement of some variables requires moderate levels of inference, such measures are more subject to random error. Relevant information is also missing more often, and therefore you are unlikely to be able to code some of the cases in the sample. In addition, as noted above, when variables require moderate levels of inference, coders usually agree with each other less often. Bradley (1989) presents evidence that coding the gender division of labor in agriculture requires moderate inference. Other examples of variables that require a moderate degree of inference include: the proportion of the day an infant is carried (J. W. M. Whiting 1981) and war frequency (C. R. Ember and M. Ember 1992a; Ross 1983). For moderate-inference variables, coders usually have to read through a considerable amount of ethnographic material that is not explicitly quantitative in order to rate a case. Because of the imprecision, the coding decision is more likely to contain some error, and a coder probably would not be able to code some or many of the cases.

The highest degree of inference is required when researchers are interested in assessing general attitudes or global concepts such as "evaluation of children" (Barry et al. 1977). What is critical is the fact that such global concepts do not have obvious empirical referents to guide coders, and so coders focusing upon different domains might code the same society differently. The most appropriate solution here, we believe, is to develop a series of more specific measures with clear empirical referents, as Whyte (1978) did for the various meanings of women's status and Ross (1983) did for the various dimensions of political decision-making and conflict. This means that instead of asking coders to evaluate if boys are preferred to girls, you might ask more specific questions. Is there any special birth celebration for a male infant? a female infant? Is there any stated preference for a male or female child? Is there any statement that parents are disappointed when a male child or a female child is born? Is there any evidence that parents are more likely to practice infanticide on one sex or the other? Is there a stigma attached to a woman who does not have a male child? a female child? A code sheet can be developed for recording the answers to the different questions. Afterward, you can always combine the particular answers to construct a more general measure. Leave room for the unexpected; be prepared to revise your coding rules to accommodate unanticipated information. And even if you decide to ask for an overall evaluation from the coder, these specific pieces of information can be checked against the overall assessment. In other words, we are suggesting that you try to transform higher inference variables into lower inference variables.

If higher inference codings are desired despite their greater potential for error, it is especially important that you ask coders to write down the reasons for their inferences. They should be asked to record quotations that are relevant, so that their scale point judgments can be checked by others later.

It is fairly obvious that the lower the inference required, the less room there is for systematic or random error. Whyte (1978) illustrates this very well when he tested for systematic errors by gender of coders as well as ethnographers (we discuss how to do this later). Overall, Whyte found very little evidence of bias in more than fifty-two variables—hardly more than would be expected by chance. And the codes showing the possibility of bias tended to involve judgments that were more abstract (e.g., women are believed to be generally inferior to men).

Time and Place Foci

Unless you are trying to assess time-lagged effects, it is important to measure your hypothetically related variables for the same time and place in a given sample case. Otherwise, you may be introducing random error that will wash out the real relationship. Divale (1975), acting on our suggestion, has shown with a few examples how lack of time and place focus, which presumably increases random error, tends to lower correlations. The same time and place for a sample case should be attended to whether previous or newly developed codes are used. Consider the following example. Melvin Ember (1974, 1984/85) has presented evidence that polygyny (allowing men to have more than one wife at the same time) is favored by a shortage of men because of high male mortality in war. If polygyny was present in a particular society as of 1900, but you measured the sex ratio in a later ethnography (after warfare ceased), you would be likely to find a more or less balanced sex ratio at the later time. Would this case be exceptional to the theory that high male mortality (and an excess of women) favors polygyny? The answer of course is not really, because it would not be appropriate to measure the two variables in this way. The two variables should be measured synchronically (i.e., for more or less the same time), or you could measure male mortality in war or the sex ratio for a slightly earlier time than you measure form of marriage. Otherwise, you may be introducing so much measurement error that the relationship between excess women and polygyny could be masked. (If you want to use previous researchers' coded data, C. R. Ember's [1992] concordance between cross-cultural samples can help you match time and place foci across samples.) Requiring that your measurements on each case pertain to the same time and place, or the appropriate relative times for a diachronic (over time) test, can only maximize your chances of seeing a relationship that truly exists.

A sample case may be described by more than one ethnographer. How should you pick your time focus? There are a number of different strategies—no one is a perfect solution.

1. Decide on the basis of the research problem. If you want to study some phenomenon that has tended to disappear in recent times (such as native religious beliefs), you might specify the earliest time period described; if you are interested in the interaction of modern medicine and traditional medicine, you might choose a more recent period. Or, if you are interested in culture change, you might want to contrast an early and a late time period. Remember that you will need information on all the variables for most of your sample cases, so you should choose a time period for a case that has at least one fairly comprehensive ethnography or a lot of other descriptive documents.

2. Decide on a time and place focus according to which ethnographer devotes the most or clearest attention to the topic you are most interested in. If you are concerned that you might be biased in deciding this way, ask someone else to choose the focal ethnographer, or use an objective criterion such as number of pages devoted to the topic of most interest to you. For example, many ethnographers do not pay that much attention to children's behavior and activities. If you require a considerable amount of information about childhood, consider choosing on the basis of which time or place has the most coverage of childhood. If there is more than one time period with considerable information, randomly choose the focal time period. To avoid bias, it is always preferable to pick the time and place focus prior to actually reading the ethnography and coding the variables.

3. If you are going to be using information from another sample to measure one or more of your variables, use the time and place focus specified in that other sample.

Minimizing the Effect of Ethnographer (or Informant) Error

So far the steps we have suggested in research design may minimize some kinds of error. But there are some errors that seem to be beyond our control. If someone hides or distorts the truth, is there anything we can do about it? If an ethnographer idealizes a situation, such as reporting traditional drinks but not the regular consumption of a cola soft drink, what can we do?

In collecting data in the field, there are techniques for checking on a person's accuracy. The most important way is by collecting data with different methods. In cross-cultural research using ethnography, the situation is somewhat different. If there was only one ethnographer in the time and place you are interested in, there is no way to check on accuracy unless you have access to a time machine. Some famous disagreements between ethnographers seemed at first to involve questions of accuracy, but were probably due to the ethnographers having done their fieldwork at different times (e.g., Oscar Lewis versus Robert Redfield about social conditions in Tepotzlan, Mexico) or at different times as well as different places (John Fisher versus Ward Goodenough about residence patterns in Truk; Derek Freeman versus Margaret Mead about sexual life in Samoa). We should expect ethnographers to differ often if their time and place foci are different, because different localities in a society can vary, often considerably, and cultures are likely to change over time (M. Ember 1985).

Just how serious is error by ethnographers? The supposedly poor or uneven quality of the ethnographic record is often mentioned as invalidating cross-cultural research. The notion is that results can't be trusted because the original data are untrustworthy. This notion is puzzling, given that ethnographers don't usually question the accuracy of their own work. If most anthropologists have high regard for the ethnography they themselves produce, and if they are correct in that regard, how could the bulk of ethnography be untrustworthy (C. R. Ember 1986: 2)? Surely there are errors in the ethnographic record and we must try to minimize their effects, but the critics' worry may derive from their ignorance about the effect of error on results. As we have seen, a great deal of error is most unlikely to produce a statistically significant finding. Even double systematic error would not normally produce a statistically significant finding that was in fact false. (Of course, there is always the possibility of deliberate cheating; but this probably does not happen often and other investigators' attempts to replicate a result will eventually reveal cheating.) Given that random error generally reduces the magnitude of observed correlations, more error lessens the likelihood of finding patterns that are really out there. And if error makes us *less* likely to infer statistical significance, it cannot be that significant cross-cultural results are generally invalid. It may seem paradoxical, but the more random error there is, the more likely the "true" results are even better than the observed results!

We may not be able to correct error in ethnography, but we can do things to minimize the possibility that it will mask true relations and differences, or make a false result look true. We should be more concerned about the possibility of missing things, that we will not see a relationship. This is the main reason we should try to minimize the effect of ethnographer (or informant) error.

Data Quality Checks

Naroll (1962, 1970b) proposed an indirect method—"data quality control"—for testing for systematic informant and ethnographer errors. His basic procedure involved identifying general factors that might produce biases in the reporting of certain variables (for example, a short stay in the field would presumably make for underreporting of "secret" practices such as witchcraft) and then testing to see if these factors correlate with the variables of interest. Indeed, Naroll found that short-staying ethnographers were significantly less likely to report witchcraft than long-staying ethnographers. Such a finding suggests the possibility of systematic error due to length of stay—short-staying ethnographers may not be told about activities that the people frown upon. Hence short-staying ethnographers may systematically underreport witchcraft. Of course, the significant correlation with length of stay may not indicate systematic error at all. As Naroll (1962) himself was aware, there are other possible interpretations of the correlation. One is that short stays may be more likely in complex cultures. If more complex cultures are less likely to have witchcraft beliefs than less complex cultures, the correlation between length of stay and the presence of witchcraft would be spurious, not due to systematic underreporting by short-staying ethnographers.

Naroll urged cross-cultural researchers to control statistically on data-quality variables (e.g., length of stay in the field), to see if they might account for results. But there are two reasons to disagree with this injunction. First, as Naroll (1977) also noted, it is very expensive to code for a large number of features that could, but probably do not, produce false correlations. Second, of the large number of studies done by Naroll, his students, and others (see Levinson 1978 for substantive studies using data quality controls), few have found that a data quality feature accounts for a correlation (but see Rohner et al. 1973; Divale 1976). Therefore, C. R. Ember et al. (1991) recommend that before investigating relationships between data quality variables and substantive variables, researchers should have plausible theoretical reasons for thinking they may be related. If we can't imagine how a data quality variable could explain a correlation, it probably isn't necessary to spend time and money coding for it. Only plausible alternative predictors should be built into a research design. However, C. R. Ember et al. (1991) do recommend that researchers develop a specific data quality code for each substantive variable (for each case), to provide a direct assessment of the quality of the data in regard to that variable. Researchers could then look to see if results with lower quality data are weaker than results with higher quality data.

To illustrate how a specific data quality code for a variable can help you find higher quality data, suppose you were trying to measure the frequency of extended family households and you compared four different ethnographers. The first had only one sentence dealing with type of family, which said: "The typical household consists of a man and his wife, his married sons and their wives and children." The second also had only one sentence: "In the census that I undertook in the village, 45 percent of the households had at least two constituent families united by a blood tie." The third had a whole chapter on families in the village. There were four case studies of families. One of them was described as consisting of parents, a married daughter and her husband, and their young children. Two of the others were composed of a husband and wife with young children, and the fourth was a widowed wife with her teenage children. Although a whole chapter was devoted to families, nothing was said about any general tendencies. The fourth ethnographer said, "A three-generational household is the ideal household form."

The cross-cultural researcher could try to minimize error by instructing the coders not to make frequency judgments based on statements about what people prefer ("ideal culture") or when the ethnographer does not give any indication of general tendency. Another strategy (or an additional strategy) is to use the information available, but score the quality of data in terms of a scale designed for this particular variable. For example, a data-quality control score might look like this:

1. Ethnographer provides evidence that the type of household was explicitly counted in a survey or census. Frequency can be judged by ethnographer's summary of that census or by browsing the census.
2. Ethnographer had a general, but nonquantitative, statement of frequency or prevalence and provided details indicating that the topic was of more than passing interest to the ethnographer.
3. Ethnographer had a general, but nonquantitative, statement with no supporting details or with no indication that the topic of family was of more than passing interest.
4. Ethnographer had no summary statement of actual frequency, only a statement dealing with ideal culture.

5. Ethnographer had no summary statement or quantitative information; anecdotes or examples of family life were given.

Using these data quality codes, let us code the sentences above:

- The first had only one sentence dealing with type of family, which said: "The typical household consists of a man and his wife, his married sons and their wives and children." This would be given a data quality score of "3."
- The second also had only one sentence. "In the census that I undertook in the village, 45 percent of the households had at least two constituent families united by a blood tie." This would be given a data quality score of "1."
- The third had a whole chapter on families in the village. There were four case studies of families. Although a whole chapter was devoted to families, nothing was said about any general tendencies. This would be given a data quality score of "5."
- The fourth said "A three-generational household is the ideal household form." This would be given a data quality score of "4."

What you include in the data quality code would depend on the variable being measured. That is, the nature of the variable would dictate what could be considered good quality data. If the variable we are trying to measure is the frequency or prevalence of extended family households, we are not so much concerned with how long the ethnographer was there, or whether the ethnographer was especially interested in families. We are mostly interested in whether the data presented allow us to be fairly certain that the ethnographer's information gives us the correct answer. Clearly, the ethnographer who had a whole chapter on families was interested in family life. The problem is that the information provided is not that informative about our variable. We know that there is one extended family out of the four, but do we take that as the typical frequency? We think doing so is more problematic than taking the statement about the ideal pattern. However, if we were constructing a data quality control code about socialization practices, such as whether parents practice physical punishment, we might want to weigh ethnographer interest in parents and children more. So, for example, we might want to give a higher data quality control score to an ethnographer who had a chapter on growing up than to an ethnographer who had only a single paragraph on child rearing.

These data quality scores would allow us to check on the possible influence of data quality on our results. For example, with a data quality code by case for each variable, we could analyze the results with *and* without the "poorer" quality data. Since the chances are greater that the scores with poor quality data will have more error, both random and systematic, the omission of cases with poor-quality data should generally yield stronger results than a data set including poor-quality data. If, by any chance, the results improve with poorer quality data, that would suggest the possibility of double systematic bias producing a falsely positive result.

We think the data quality control procedure suggested here provides two important advantages. First, it taps the quality of the ethnographic information more directly than Naroll's suggested strategy, which may not make any difference at all in regard to a particular correlation. Second, the data quality coding we suggest can be done quite efficiently, at the same time substantive variables are coded, because reading additional material is not required.

Inferring the Absence of a Trait and the Problem of Missing Data

Cross-cultural researchers have to deal with another problem in the ethnographic record, the problem of "missing data." In addition to errors in what is reported, there are things that may not be reported. Ethnographers may not have gone to the field with a comprehensive guide to what kinds of information could be collected, such as is provided by the *Outline of Cultural Materials* (Murdock et al. 2000). For this and other reasons, ethnographers often pay little or no attention to a question that is of interest later to the cross-cultural researcher. What should the cross-culturalist do? We do not recommend inferring that something is absent if it is not reported, unless the cross-cultural researcher can be quite sure that it would have been reported if it had been present. For example, if an ethnographer did not mention puberty rites but thoroughly discussed childhood and adolescence, the cross-cultural researcher could reasonably infer the absence of puberty rites. If, however, the ethnographer did not collect any information on adolescence, the fact that no puberty rites are mentioned should not be taken to mean that they were absent. Researchers need to specify coding rules for inferring absence (see the measure of extended family households described above) or they need to instruct their coders not to make inferences in the absence of directly relevant evidence.

Another strategy that can be used to deal with the problem of missing data is to interview the original ethnographers themselves (or others who have worked for extended periods in the society) to supplement the information not present in the published sources (Levinson 1989; Pryor 1977; Ross 1983). The cross-cultural researcher has to be careful to keep to the same time and place foci to which the published data pertain; if you call or write to a recent ethnographer about a case, you should ask only about the time and place focus of the published information you want to use.

Finally, if data on some of the sample societies are missing, the cross-cultural researcher may decide to impute missing values. Burton (1996) has described and evaluated a number of procedures for doing so. The cross-cultural researcher needs to bear in mind that any method of imputation is likely to increase measurement error. Therefore the advantage of imputation (to increase sample size) has to be weighed carefully against the possible increase of error. Researchers who impute some data should consider doing analyses with and without the imputed data to see if the imputing has misleadingly improved the results, just as we can compare data sets with and without dubious codings to see if including them has transformed a borderline or nonsignificant result into a significant one.

Minimizing Coder Error

The coding process itself can produce measurement error. If the investigator is also the coder, there is the possibility of systematic bias in favor of the theory being tested (Rosenthal 1966; Rosenthal and Jacobson 1968). For that reason alone many researchers prefer to use "naive" or theory-blind coders. However, naive coders may not be as likely as experienced coders to make accurate judgments. Experienced researchers have skills that should make for more accurate coding, because they are more likely to be aware that an ethnographer's words should not always be taken at face value. For example, an experienced researcher is more likely to know that avunculocal residence might be called patrilocal residence and that hunter-gatherers may get plenty of food (even if they have to move their camps frequently, that doesn't necessarily mean their food supply is precarious). Furthermore, experienced coders are more likely to pay attention to time and place foci—to know that when one ethnographer describes what Samoans do, he may not be talking about the particular time period or particular group of Samoans a previous ethnographer has studied and described (M. Ember 1985).

Bradley (1987) argues that naive coders can make systematic errors when coding instructions are insufficiently precise, especially when coding high-inference variables. For example, differences between her codes for the division of labor in agriculture and those of the coders for Murdock and Provost (1973) could be explained by the possibility that the Murdock and Provost coders were not instructed to consider differences between crop types or which phase of the agricultural sequence was to be coded. Naive coders might also be more likely to make judgments that are systematically biased toward their own cultural assumptions, as is suggested by the experimental findings presented by D'Andrade (1974).

Researchers can try to minimize the error of inexperienced coders by being as explicit as possible in their coding instructions and by making sure that the codes do not surpass the information that is generally available in the ethnographic literature (Tatje 1970). Coding should require as few inferential leaps as possible. The process of trying to spell out all the possible obstacles to coding is an important part of the research design. It may be that having at least one relatively inexperienced coder provides an advantage—it may force the researcher to be as clear as possible in the operationalization of theoretical concepts.

People who are not cross-culturalists (and even some who are) may worry that coders will introduce systematic errors because of their gender, their political ideology, their personality, or their faulty assumptions about different types of societies. But such contamination may not be so likely. Whyte (1978) did not find more significant relationships between gender of coder and his many indicators of women's status than would be expected by chance. His research suggests that systematic coding bias is most likely to occur when codes are very general (requiring a high degree of inference), which may allow the coder's personal background to exert an influence on the coding process. Whyte suggests that personal/cultural biases can be avoided if coders are asked to rate concrete or specific customs and behaviors. If you are asked to code specific kinds of behavior, there is less chance that your general expectations (right or wrong) will affect your judgments.

Designing studies to test systematically for coder biases is normally quite expensive, because to do so properly requires more than one coder for each "bias type." Thus, it is more cost-effective for the investigator and a naive coder to rate the cases. Not only could we then compare the two sets of ratings for reliability, we could also see if both sets of ratings give similar results. If they do not, that would be something to be concerned with. It might only be that the naive coder's ratings contained more error; the results using only that coder's ratings should be weaker than the results using only the investigator's ratings. Perhaps the best strategy is to test hypotheses using only those cases that both raters agreed on. That way, you would probably be omitting the cases with more random error.

In chapter 9 (after we discuss statistical analysis), we discuss how to assess the reliability of codings and what to do about disagreements among coders.

6

Sampling

A ll researchers sample, whether they intend to or not. And not just cross-cultural researchers. Even fieldwork involves sampling. When the anthropologist decides to study a particular culture in the field, he or she picks that culture out of the larger universe of all existing cultures. And when the field researcher gets to the field, she or he has to decide on the community in which to live and work. But why is that community picked? Frank Young (personal communication) recounted that early in his career he and his wife decided to visit the communities in Mexico that had been studied by other anthropologists. After visiting them all, he couldn't quite put his finger on what was similar about them. But he finally realized what it was—all the villages were picturesque! If Young was correct, the previous anthropologists' field sites probably do not constitute an unbiased sample of Mexican communities. Rather the choices were probably biased toward qualities that appealed to the anthropologists.

A satisfactory sample should represent a larger universe of cases in a fair or representative way so that we can generalize the sample results to the larger universe from which the sample was drawn. To do this, we must adopt a sampling procedure that is not based on subjective criteria. In this chapter we discuss a variety of **probability sampling** techniques. With probability sampling, each case has a known (and nonzero) chance of being chosen. In the simplest probability sample, all cases have an equal chance to be chosen (**simple random sampling**). We study a sample because we can't study the entire universe, or it would be prohibitively expensive to do so.

Let's define some terms. The universe of cases one wants to generalize to is called a **population.** A population can be any set of units or cases. We are most used to thinking of populations as comprising individual people. Such a population may be as broad as all people in the world or as narrow as all registered voters in a Connecticut city. But the cases in a statistical population don't have to be individuals. They could be families, households, communities, societies, countries, and so on. They could be events or activities. They could be anything. The units actually studied (of whatever type) are the sampling units or **units of analysis.** While the population is what you want to generalize to, in practical terms it is usually necessary to have a written list or some other way of identifying the sampling units (such as an aerial map of the houses in a community).[1] The list of units is called the **sampling frame.** When we sample, then, we select cases from a sampling frame (cf. M. Ember and C. R. Ember n.d.).

While it may seem that it would always be better to study all the cases, rather than just some, sampling theorists suggest otherwise. There are two main reasons why sampling is preferable to studying all the cases (Kalton 1983). The first reason is that sampling is more economical. If you study some of the people in a community rather than all of the people, you save time and money for other research purposes. The second reason to sample is that you might actually get higher quality data by studying fewer people.[2] Research always takes longer than expected. Suppose you have two assistants in a community of 1,000 adults. To investigate everyone, each assistant would have to interview 500. If time is running out, they might rush and not do a thorough job. If you decided to investigate a 10 percent sample (100 of the 1,000 adults), each assistant would have only fifty adults to interview and they might be more careful. Besides, if everyone were interviewed, people might start to compare the questions and answers, possibly contaminating the results. If you were to hire more assistants, that would make the study more expensive. And some of the additional assistants might not be as well trained as the others or you may not have enough time to supervise them all adequately. In short, there are good reasons to sample a population.

It is rarely necessary to sample a large proportion of cases from the sampling frame. Political opinion polling is a case in point. The number of voters in the United States is a very large number. Yet very accurate results can be obtained by randomly sampling a few hundred to a few thousand potential voters. In the 1992 election of President Clinton, almost all major public opinion polls predicted the percent of votes for Clinton to within one percentage point. Yet, the number of individuals sampled ranged from only 722 to 9,115![3] The most important factor in correct predictions is not the size of the sample, but the method of sampling.

Sampling issues for cross-cultural comparisons are mostly like the issues in polling. The ethnographic record as a whole is too big to be studied entirely and doing so would take enormous effort and expense. But how many cases should be selected for comparison and how should they be selected? As we will see, some kind of probability sampling is the sampling method of choice.

Exactly how you draw the sample depends on the purpose of the research. If the purpose is to answer a descriptive question about incidence or frequency in the world or in a region, then it is critical that all the cases (countries or cultures) be listed in the sampling frame and that all have an equal chance to be chosen (the major reason sample results can be generalized to the larger universe of cases). Otherwise, you cannot claim that the sample results are generalizable to any larger population of cases. How large the sample should be (see below) depends on many factors, but an important one is how accurate you need to be. If a political contest is very close and you do not want to call the election incorrectly, you will need a much larger sample than if two candidates are ten points apart. In the first situation, an error of 1 percent may be disastrous for correct prediction; in the second situation, an error of as much as 4 percent will not make a difference in the outcome. Cross-culturally, how large the sample should be also depends in part on how accurate you need to be. If you want to discover whether or not babies typically sleep in the same bed as their parents, a large sample is not so important. But if you need an accurate measure of fertility to estimate future population growth, a figure that is off by a few percentage points can lead to a very incorrect prediction.

SAMPLING IN COMPARISONS USING PRIMARY DATA

There have been relatively few comparisons using primary data (collected by the researcher in two or more field sites) in anthropology. In cross-cultural psychology, the situation is different; there are a considerable number of two-case comparisons, usually comparing subjects in the United States with subjects in some other place. Generally, if not always, the sampling in comparisons using primary data has been purposive and not based on probability methods. This is understandable, given the political realities of gaining permission to do fieldwork in certain countries. Given the cost of fieldwork, it is also not surprising that two-case comparisons are more common than any other kind of comparison using primary data. Unfortunately, the scientific value of two-case comparisons is dubious. Years ago, Donald Campbell (1961: 344) pointed out that a difference between two cases could be explained by *any* other difference(s) between the cases. Let us consider a hypothetical example.

Assume we are comparing two societies with different levels of fertility. We may think that the difference is due to a greater need for child labor in one society because there is more agricultural and household work to be done in that society. As plausible as this theory may sound, we should be skeptical about it because many other differences between the two societies could actually be responsible for the difference in fertility. The high-fertility society may also have earlier weaning, a shorter postpartum sex taboo, better medical care, and so on. Using aggregate or cultural data on the two societies, you cannot rule out the possibility that some of the other known differences (and still others not known) may be responsible for the difference in fertility. If, however, you have data on a sample of mothers in each society, and measures of fertility and the possible causes of differential fertility for each sample mother, we could do statistical analyses (e.g., multiple regression analyses) that would allow us to narrow down the causal possibilities in each society. Then, of course, you have more than a two-case comparison, because you would be comparing mothers. (And if the two societies showed the same results, your confidence in the results would be enhanced.) The point here is that comparing just two cases cannot tell you what may be accounting for the differences between them.

So what is the minimum number of cases (societies) for a comparative test using primary data? If two variables are related, the minimum number of cases that might provide a statistically significant result—assuming unbiased sampling, errorless measurement, and a hypothesis that is true—is four (cf. R. L. Munroe and R. H. Munroe 1991b); but the result (e.g., a correlation) has to be extraordinarily strong (close to perfect). Examples of four-case comparisons that use primary data and that employ theoretically derived criteria for case selection are the four-culture project on culture and ecology in East Africa, directed by Walter Goldschmidt (1965), and the Munroes' four-culture project on socialization (R. H. Munroe et al. 1984; R. L. Munroe and R. H. Munroe 1992). In the East Africa project, which was concerned with the effect of ecology/economy on personality and social life, two communities (one pastoral and one agricultural) in each of four cultures (two Kalenjin-speaking and two Bantu-speaking) were selected. The Munroes selected four cultures from around the world to examine the effects of variation in degree of father-absence and in degree of male-centered social structure.

SAMPLING IN COMPARISONS USING SECONDARY DATA

First you have to decide what your sampling frame is, what list of cases you want to generalize the sample results to. Is it to be worldwide (all countries or all societies)? Is it to be regional? (A broad region like North America, or a narrower region like the cultures of the American Southwest?). In specifying your sampling frame, you are also specifying your unit of analysis. A country is not necessarily equivalent to a society or culture in the anthropological sense. A country (or nation-state) is a politically unified population; it may, and often does, contain more than one culture or society, anthropologically speaking. Conventionally, a culture is the set of customary beliefs and practices characteristic of a society, the latter being the population that occupies a particular territory and speaks a common language not generally understood by neighboring populations. Once it is clear what the researcher wants to generalize the sample results to, the researcher should sample from a list containing all the eligible cases. Cross-national researchers have no problem constructing a list of countries. Cross-cultural researchers do not yet have a complete list of the world's described cultures, although such a list is currently under construction at HRAF headquarters at Yale. But there are large lists of cultures to sample from.

Several published lists of societies have served as sampling frames for most cross-cultural studies; a few of them claim to accurately represent the world's cultures, but we argue below that these claims are problematic. Therefore, cross-cultural researchers cannot yet generalize sample results to all cultures. Any claim about a relationship or about the proportion of societies that have a particular trait should be tempered by the recognition that the generalization is only applicable to the list sampled from, and only if the particular cases investigated constitute an unbiased sample of the larger list.

Currently available cross-cultural samples, which have served as sampling frames, include the following (from largest to smallest—see table 6.1):

1. The "Ethnographic Atlas" (1962ff., beginning in *Ethnology* 1 [1962]: 113ff. and continuing intermittently over succeeding years and issues of the journal), with a total of 1,264 cases;
2. The "Summary" version of the "Ethnographic Atlas" (Murdock 1967), with a total of 862 cases;
3. The "World Ethnographic Sample" (Murdock 1957), with 565 cases;
4. The *Atlas of World Cultures* (Murdock 1981), with 563 cases;
5. The annually growing HRAF Collection of Ethnography (see the appendix), which covered more than 365 cultures as of 2000. (The HRAF sample is a collection of full texts grouped by culture and indexed by topic for quick information retrieval; no precoded data are provided for the sample cases, in contrast to the situation for all of the other samples except item 6.)

6. The "Standard Ethnographic Sample, Second Edition" (Naroll and Sipes 1973 and addenda in Naroll and Zucker 1974), with 273 cases;
7. The "Standard Cross-Cultural Sample" (Murdock and White 1969), with 186 cases;
8. The "HRAF Probability Sample" (Naroll 1967; HRAF 1967; Lagacé 1979), with 60 cases. (This sample is also called the "HRAF Quality Control Sample," for which some precoded data are available; each sample case was randomly selected from a different culture area in the world.)

Before we turn to examine some of the claims made about these various samples, we need first to realize why it is important to use probability sampling procedures, particularly random sampling.

According to sampling theory, only *random* sampling provides an unbiased or representative sample of some larger population or sampling frame (Cochran 1977: 8–11; see also Kish 1987: 16). For example, simple random sampling (using a table of random numbers or a "lottery" type of selection procedure) guarantees that every case in the sampling frame has had an equal chance to be chosen. (Equal probability of selection is assumed in most tests that estimate the statistical significance, or likely truth-value, of sample results.) To sample in a simple random fashion, all you have to do is make sure that all cases in the sampling frame are numbered uniquely (no repeats, no cases omitted). Researchers may sometimes opt for other kinds of probability sampling, such as systematic sampling (every nth case is chosen after a random start) or stratified sampling (first dividing the sample into subgroups or strata and then randomly sampling from each).

There are two kinds of stratified sampling. In **proportionate stratified sampling**, each subgroup is represented in proportion to its occurrence in the total population; in **disproportionate stratified sampling**, some subgroups are overrepresented and others are underrepresented. Disproportionate stratified sampling is used in cross-cultural research when the researcher needs to overrepresent a rare type of case in order to have enough such cases to study (as in a comparison of relatively rare hunter-gatherers with more common agriculturalists) or when a researcher wants to derive an accurate estimate of some parameter (e.g., mean, variance, or strength of an association) for a rare subgroup. If probability methods are used to sample within each stratum, proportionate stratified sampling gives every case an equal chance to be chosen. Disproportionate sampling, however, does not give equal weight to each case. Researchers need to be careful not to generalize to a larger population from a disproportionate sample. It should be noted that stratified sampling may not improve much on the accuracy obtainable with a simple random sample (Kish 1987: 33).

Table 6.1. Available Cross-Cultural Samples

Name of Sample	No. of Cases	Time and Place Focus	Sampling Method	Stratified	Advantages[1]	Disadvantages[2]	Availability in Electronic Format
"Ethnographic Atlas" (1962–1967)[3]	1,264	Yes, usually	Attempted to be exhaustive[4]	No, but cases are classified by 60 areas	• Large list approximates a sampling frame • Considerable number of coded variables	• Considerable splitting of cases in North America • Corrections made subsequently in print hard to find (but see next column) • Bibliography must be obtained from original issues of *Ethnology*	• Corrected Codes available from the electronic journal *World Cultures* • Coded data from *World Cultures* is planned for the future on the HRAF home page
"Ethnographic Atlas: A Summary" (1967)	862	Yes, usually	Judgmental winnowing of less well described cases from larger "Atlas"	No, but cases are classified into 412 clusters with an estimated divergence of at least 1,000 years	• Still a large list to sample from • Considerable number of coded variables	• Judgmental winnowing • Bibliography must be obtained from original issues of *Ethnology*	• Only as part of the whole "Atlas"

Table 6.1. Continued

Name of Sample	No. of Cases	Time and Place Focus	Sampling Method	Stratified	Advantages[1]	Disadvantages[2]	Availability in Electronic Format
"World Ethnographic Sample" (1957)	565	No	Judgmental. Criteria used: most populous, best described, representing each type of basic economy, language, distinctive culture	Disproportionate nonrandom sampling. 5 to 15 cases chosen from each of 60 culture areas	• None	• Judgmental criteria • No focus on time and place • No bibliography provided	No
Atlas of World Cultures (1981)	563	Yes, almost always	Judgmental	Yes Disproportionate. Usually 5 examples for each of 150 areas (25 areas in of each 6 world regions)	• Considerable amount of coded material provided in the same book with bibliography • Corrections from "Ethnographic Atlas" are probably incorporated	• Judgmental criteria for selection	No

Table 6.1. *Continued*

Name of Sample	No. of Cases	Time and Place Focus	Sampling Method	Stratified	Advantages[1]	Disadvantages[2]	Availability in Electronic Format
HRAF Collection of Ethnography (Human Relations Area Files 1949–)	365 in 2000; annually growing	Usually many foci for each culture[5]	• Cases will be added by simple random sampling beginning in 2000 • Past selections were judgmental[6]	No	• Extensive subject-indexing of original ethnographic works greatly facilitates measuring and coding variables • Some updating of ethnography in print and microfiche versions • All culture files converted to electronic form have been updated	• Judgmental criteria for selection prior to 2000 (but see HRAF Probability Sample Files below) • No coded variables; researchers who want to use already coded variables need to link HRAF cases to other samples[7]	• As of 2000, 78 cultures are available on the Web (or CD) at member institutions • Information about the collection is available at www.yale.edu/hraf/

Table 6.1. *Continued*

Name of Sample	No. of Cases	Time and Place Focus	Sampling Method	Stratified	Advantages[1]	Disadvantages[2]	Availability in Electronic Format
"Standard Ethnographic Sample, Second Edition" (1973)	273	Focused by ethnographer (usually is a time and place focus)	Attempt to select all "primitive tribes" that met certain data quality controls[8]	No	• None	• Researcher may not want to avoid cultures with written languages • Has no associated codes	• No
"Standard Cross-Cultural Sample" (1969)	186	Yes, almost always	Judgmental selection of 1 case per cluster, selected because of supposedly superior ethnographic coverage (as of 1969)	Yes, into 200 clusters, but not all clusters have a representative	• Many available codes on a large variety of subjects	• Judgmental selection	• Many of the variables coded for this sample are available in *World Cultures*

Table 6.1. Continued

Name of Sample	No. of Cases	Time and Place Focus[5]	Sampling Method	Stratified	Advantages[1]	Disadvantages[2]	Availability in Electronic Format
HRAF Probability Sample Files (PSF)	60 (40 additional substitute cases available)	Usually many foci for each culture[5]	Random selection from cases meeting data quality criteria[9]	Yes 60 culture areas used following the "Ethnographic Atlas Summary" with slight changes	• Provides a form of random sampling • Extensive subject-indexing of original ethnographic works greatly facilitates measuring and coding new variables • Updated cultural files now on the Web • Some coded data available from HRAF	• If a large number of cases is needed to test a hypothesis, sample size is limited. However, additional PSF cases are available	• The Probability Sample Files (plus additional cultures) are available on the Web (or CD) at member institutions • Information about the collection is available at www.yale.edu/hraf/

1. Unless otherwise noted under Disadvantages, the sample contains bibliography.
2. Unless otherwise noted under Advantages, the sample has not been updated.
3. Originally published in the journal *Ethnology* from 1962ff. A corrected print version edited by J. Patrick Gray is planned (to be published by AltaMira Press).

Table 6.1. *Continued*

4. Murdock admitted that it was far from exhaustive for east Eurasia, the insular Pacific, and Europe.

5. Because each culture file usually contains the work of more than one ethnographer, there will usually be data for more than one time period and more than one location. The foci can usually be obtained in the 111 category of the paper and microfiche collection and on the Web following each abstract at the beginning of each document. HRAF also publishes a database (C. R. Ember 1992) that identifies the various documents pertaining to the same time and place focus (see the section in chapter 4 on time and place focus for more explanation.)

6. The HRAF staff tried to pick cases that were well described across a broad range of subjects and to minimize too many cases from any one culture area. Funding considerations also influenced some of the cultures chosen. The Probability Sample Files is a special subset—see below.

7. The database contained in *Computerized Concordance of Cross-Cultural Samples* (C. R. Ember 1992) identifies cases that match time and place foci across samples. Alternative names are also given for different samples. So, for example, if a researcher wants to find the sources to use in HRAF that were used by Murdock in the Ethnographic Atlas, the concordance identifies the document numbers in HRAF that conform to the Atlas. This is the same for all the other samples in the chart above.

8. These criteria included (1) at least one ethnographer who lived there for more than one year; (2) an ethnographer who had a working knowledge of the native language; (3) an ethnographer with at least forty published pages dealing with at least ten of the seventy-nine major categories in the *Outline of Cultural Materials*, and (4) the absence of a native, written language.

9. This sample, which was devised by Raoul Naroll and executed by the HRAF staff in 1967, first identified all the cultures that fulfilled the following criteria: (1) at least 2,400 pages of ethnography to be listed on the "A" list (1,200 pages to be listed on the "B" list); (2) substantial contributions by at least two authors; (3) accounts considered reliable by the profession; (4) coverage on at least forty of the major topical categories (the 2-digit categories) in the *Outline of Cultural Materials*. If there was more than one case on the "A" list, one was randomly chosen first. If none was on the "A" list, a case was randomly chosen from the "B" list.

Systematic sampling may be preferred because it is a little easier than simple random sampling, which requires you to list and number all of the cases in the sampling frame and then look down a table of random numbers to find the sample cases. Like simple random sampling, it also gives every case an equal chance to be chosen. Although it is easier to choose cases by systematic sampling, it has a major disadvantage. Once a decision is made to study every *n*th case, it is necessary to proceed through the entire list. Otherwise, your sample will not be representative of the entire sampling frame. With simple random sampling, you can look down the table of random numbers and stop as soon as you have found the desired number of sample cases.

Comparing the Available Cross-Cultural Samples

Three of the existing cross-cultural samples were said to be relatively complete lists when they were published. The largest is the complete "Ethnographic Atlas" (with 1,264 cases), published from 1962 on in the journal *Ethnology*. But, as its compiler (Murdock 1967: 109) noted, not even the Atlas is an exhaustive list of what he called the "adequately described" cultures; he acknowledged that East Eurasia, the Insular Pacific, and Europe were not well represented in the Atlas. For the smaller "summary" version of the Atlas (Murdock 1967), he dropped all the cases he considered poorly described. So if you want your sampling frame to include only well-described cases (in Murdock's opinion), then the 1967 Atlas Summary (with 862 cases) is a reasonable list to sample from.

Raoul Naroll set out to construct a list of societies that met his stringent criteria for eligibility. Some of his criteria were: the culture had to lack a native written language; it had to have an ethnographer who lived for at least a year in the field; and the ethnographer had to know the native language. The resultant sample, which he called the "Standard Ethnographic Sample" (Naroll and Sipes 1973; see also Naroll and Zucker 1974), contains 285 societies; Naroll and Sipes claimed that this list was about 80 to 90 percent complete for the cultures that qualified at the time (eastern Europe and East Asia were admittedly underrepresented).

None of these lists has been updated. A more complete list of the world's described cultures is under development at the Human Relations Area Files under the direction of Carol R. Ember and with the advice of the anthropological profession. This new list will be the sampling frame that HRAF uses, beginning in 2000, to add cases by simple random sampling to the HRAF Collection of Ethnography. Three of the existing samples (from largest to smallest: the *Atlas of World Cultures* [Murdock 1981], the "Standard Cross-Cultural Sample" [Murdock and White 1969], and the subset of HRAF called the HRAF Probability Sample Files [Naroll

1967; HRAF 1967; Lagacé 1979]) were developed to give equal weight to each of a number of culture areas (areas of similar cultures) in the world. Technically, the samples mentioned in this paragraph are all disproportionate stratified samples (only one of the three—the HRAF Probability Sample Files—employs random sampling to select cases for each culture area identified). The sampling is disproportionate from the strata because the number of cases selected for each identified culture area is not proportionate to the real number of cases in the culture area. The presumption behind all of these stratified samples is that the cultures in a given area are bound to be very similar by reason of common ancestry or extensive diffusion. The designers of these samples wanted to minimize **"Galton's Problem."** In the last section of this chapter, we discuss whether or not Galton's Problem really is a problem, as well as nonsampling solutions to the presumed problem.

There are other problems with the disproportionate stratified samples. First, exactly how many culture areas should we distinguish? This requires empirical testing. Burton et al. (1996) have shown that social structural variables do not cluster consistently with the culture areas distinguished by Murdock, which may lead some to question the presumed separateness of those areas. Second, if a culture area is not clearly differentiated from other culture areas in the frequency of traits of interest to the researcher, disproportionate stratified sampling may not provide a more efficient way to sample (more accurate, with fewer cases) than simple random sampling. Third, even if the disproportionate sample employs random sampling from each stratum, every case selected will not have had an equal chance to be chosen. This makes it difficult or impossible to estimate the commonness or uniqueness of a particular trait in the world. If we do not know how common a trait is in each culture area, we cannot correct our counts by relative weighting, which we would need to do to make an accurate estimate of the frequency of the trait in the world.

Many have used all or some of the cases in the "Standard Cross-Cultural Sample" (Murdock and White 1969) for cross-cultural studies, at least partly because the published literature contains a large number of codes (ratings of variables) on those cases; many of these codes were reprinted in Barry and Schlegel (1980). This sample is claimed to be representative of the world's known and well-described cultures (as of 1969), but that claim is dubious for two reasons. First, as already noted, disproportionate sampling does not give an equal chance for each culture to be chosen. Second, the single sample case from each cluster was chosen judgmentally, not randomly. (Judgmental criteria were also used to choose the five cases per culture area for the *Atlas of World Cultures* [Murdock 1981].)

Of the three samples discussed here, the HRAF Probability Sample Files is the only available sample employing *random* sampling within the strata (the sixty-culture sample includes one random selection from each identified culture area). However, the other criteria for selection were so stringent (e.g., at least 1,200 pages of cultural data focused on a community or other delimited unit; substantial contributions from at least two different authors) that only 206 societies in the whole world were eligible for inclusion at the time the sample was constructed in the late 1960s.

Two other samples should be briefly discussed, because some researchers have used them as sampling frames in cross-cultural studies. One is the "World Ethnographic Sample" (Murdock 1957). In addition to being based on judgmental sampling of cases within culture areas, it has one other major drawback. A time and place focus is not specified for the cases, as in the two "Ethnographic Atlas" samples (full and summary), the "Standard Cross-Cultural Sample," and the "Standard Ethnographic Sample." If researchers want to use some of the precoded data for the "World Ethnographic Sample," they would have no idea what the "ethnographic present" is for a case. As we discussed in the previous chapter, focusing on the same time and place focus for all the measures on a case is usually desirable in testing for an association; you may be introducing error if you do not make sure that the measures used for a case pertain to the same time and place.

Let us turn finally to the entire HRAF Collection of Ethnography. Like most of the other samples, it too was based on judgmental selection. But because it covers many cultures all over the world and provides full-text ethnographic materials that are complexly indexed for rapid information-retrieval, the HRAF Collection has often been used as a sampling frame for cross-cultural studies. (As of 2000, the HRAF Collection covered more than 365 cultures, at least 40 percent of the world's well-described cultures if you go by Murdock's [1967] total of 862 in the summary version of the "Ethnographic Atlas.")

The major advantage of the HRAF Collection, as compared with the other available lists or samples of cultures, is that only HRAF provides ethnographic texts on the cases. The other samples provide only coded data (usually) and only limited bibliography (usually). If the codes constructed by others do not directly measure what you are interested in, but you use them anyway, you may be reducing your chances of finding relationships and differences that truly exist in the world. Therefore, if you need to code new variables or you need to code something in a more direct way, you are likely to do better if you yourself code from the original ethnography (C. R. Ember et al. 1991). Library research to do so would be very time-consuming, which is why HRAF was invented in the first place. If you use the HRAF files, you do not have to devote weeks to constructing bibliographies for each of your

sample cases; you do not have to chase down the books and other materials you need to look at, which might have to be obtained by interli-
brary loan; and you do not have to search through every page of a
source (that often lacks an index) to find all the locations of the information you seek. The HRAF files give you the information you want on
a particular topic, from all of the sources processed for the culture, in a
convenient place. Now, with the electronic HRAF, that place is your
computer screen. If you want to examine the original ethnography on a
case (with all the context), and particularly if you want to construct
your own measures, there is no substitute for the HRAF Collection.
(See the appendix for more information on how to use the HRAF
Collections—there are two now, the Collection of Ethnography and the
Collection of Archaeology.)

So if you are starting out to do your first cross-cultural study, how
should you sample? If you want to use some of the data already coded
for one of the available samples, by all means use that sample *as your
sampling frame*, particularly if it is one of the larger lists (such as the
summary version of the "Ethnographic Atlas" [Murdock 1967]). That
sampling frame becomes the list you can generalize your results to. (A
larger claim that you are generalizing to the world would be inappropriate.) If you want to code all of your variables yourself, you can do so
most economically by sampling from the HRAF Collection of Ethnography. If a sample size of sixty is large enough, the HRAF Probability
Sample Files (which are now electronically accessible on the World
Wide Web) provide the advantage of giving you a randomly selected
case from each of Murdock's sixty world culture areas. If you want to
code some variables yourself and use some precoded variables, you can
sample from the intersection between HRAF and the sample with the
precoded variables. Whatever sampling frame you use, you should select your cases with some probability sampling method. If you want to
infer that your statistically significant sample results are probably true
for the larger universe, you should use a probability method that gives
every case an equal chance to be chosen. If for some reason you cannot
sample probabilistically from some list, you must be sure to avoid selecting the cases yourself. After a probability sample, the next best
thing is a sample that was constructed by others (who could not know
the hypotheses you want to test). Since most statistical tests assume
simple random sampling, we suggest that such a sample should be the
method of choice. The wonderful thing about a simple random sample
is that wherever your research stops, after twenty or forty or two hundred randomly selected cases, you will always be entitled to conclude
that a statistically significant result in your sample is probably true for
the larger universe.

GALTON'S PROBLEM

Some have questioned the validity of cross-cultural findings on the grounds that the samples may contain cases that are historically related. (They share a recent common origin or are near enough to each other for diffusion [cultural borrowing] to have occurred often between them.) This objection is referred to as "Galton's Problem." In 1889, Francis Galton heard Edward Tylor's presentation of what is generally considered the first cross-cultural study. Galton (see the end of Tylor 1889) suggested that many of Tylor's cases were duplicates of one another because they had similar histories, and therefore Tylor's conclusions were suspect because the sample size was unjustifiably inflated. Raoul Naroll and others have considered Galton's Problem a serious threat to cross-cultural research. They have devised several methods to test for the possible effects of diffusion and common ancestry (Naroll 1970a). The concern behind these methods is that statistical associations could not be causal if they could be attributed mostly to diffusion or common ancestry. Some cross-culturalists who were worried about Galton's Problem tried to solve it by making sure that their samples contained only one culture from a particular culture area (an area of related languages and cultures). For example, the "Standard Cross-Cultural Sample" (Murdock and White 1969) and the HRAF Probability Sample both contain only one culture per identified culture area.

How serious is Galton's Problem? Cross-culturalists disagree (see M. Ember and Otterbein 1991 for references; see also C. R. Ember 1990 and M. Ember and C. R. Ember n.d.). Most but not all cross-culturalists think that Galton's Problem is a serious problem that must be dealt with (Naroll, Schaefer, Loftin, Murdock and White, Dow—for references, see C. R. Ember 1990). Others disagree (including Strauss and Orans, Otterbein, Ember and Ember—for references, see C. R. Ember 1990; see also M. Ember and C. R. Ember n.d). Those who are not worried about Galton's Problem think that random sampling of cases is the best way to prevent sampling bias, which is what Galton and others have worried about. Also, the sample societies in most cross-cultural studies usually turn out to speak mutually unintelligible languages, which means that the speech communities involved have been separated for at least one thousand years. If two related languages began to diverge one thousand or more years ago, many other aspects of the cultures will also have diverged. Therefore such cases could hardly be duplicates of each other. If you push Galton's Problem to the limit and avoid any two cases that share a common history and language, then psychological studies with more than one individual per culture would be suspect!

We suggest that those who worry about Galton's Problem misunderstand two requirements of statistical inference: that sample cases be independent and that the measures on them should be independent (Kish 1965, 1987; Blalock 1972). Independence of cases means only that the choice of one case is not influenced by the choice of any other case (which random sampling guarantees). And the requirement of independent measurement means only that each case's score on a variable should be arrived at separately. The scores on two variables might be correlated, but that by itself doesn't violate the requirement that the measurements be made independently. For further discussion of what independence means statistically, see M. Ember and Otterbein (1991).

Until recently, whether or not you worried about Galton's Problem made a big difference in how you would do a study. Naroll's tests for the possibility of diffusion are quite time-consuming to carry out. Because they are, most cross-culturalists altered their sampling strategy to eliminate multiple cases from the same culture area. Using small random samples selected from a large list is another way to handle Galton's worry. A small random sample is unlikely to include more than a few cases, at worst, that derive from a common ancestral culture or are geographically near each other. This makes it unlikely that your sample will include duplicates. And mathematical anthropologists have recently developed statistical solutions and computer programs that treat the proximity of societies (in distance or language) as a variable whose influence can be tested in a multiple regression analysis. (This is called testing for spatial autocorrelation.[4]) Whether or not a researcher agrees that Galton's Problem is a problem, the recent mathematical and computer solutions do not require a special sampling strategy, nor do they require expensive, time-consuming controls. All you have to do, if you are concerned about Galton's Problem, is test statistically for the possibility that proximity or belonging to the same language family accounts for a result (Dow et al. 1984). Even without a statistical control for autocorrelation, cross-culturalists who randomly sample from a larger sampling frame can redo their analyses by randomly omitting more than a single case from the same culture area. If the results do not change substantially after multiple cases from an area are omitted, the original result cannot be due to duplication of cases. Indeed, it may usually be the case that duplication weakens results, because a particular set of historically related cases may be exceptional to a cross-cultural generalization rather than consistent with it (for some evidence on this possibility, see M. Ember 1971).

In short, if you are concerned about Galton's Problem, you can test for autocorrelation effects. Or you can be sure to include only one case from a culture area. Or you can use a small random sample (thirty to fifty cases) selected from a large list of societies, which will minimize the possibility of including cases that have a recent common ancestry or are near each other. Note that there is a significant possible benefit if you choose the "small random sample" way to deal with Galton's Problem. You can use the time and money you save (by not having to code variables for a large sample) to retest your results on a new small random sample. Other researchers who are worried about Galton's Problem should be reassured about the validity of your results if your results are replicated in two samples. For a guide to choosing what size sample you need, see Kraemer and Theimann (1987).

NOTES

1. Cluster sampling is one way of sampling without a prior sampling frame. You first sample geographical regions (and maybe smaller regions), then enumerate the cases within each region, and then study all or some of those cases. As far as we know, cluster sampling has not been employed in cross-cultural research.

2. This is one of the arguments made by sampling theorists regarding the census in the United States. Sampling would allow more effort to be devoted to finding individuals who are currently undercounted, such as individuals who work many jobs or who are homeless.

3. The polls were ABC (9,115 people), CNN Gallup poll (1,562), the Harris poll (1,975), the *New York Times* (2,248), the *Wall Street Journal* (982), and the *Washington Post* (722). Five of the polls predicted Clinton would get 44 percent of the vote, one predicted 43 percent. All polls predicted with a margin of error. The margin ranged from +/– 2 percent for the largest polls to +/– 4 percent for the smaller polls. The actual percentage Clinton got was 43 percent, which happened to be within 0 to 1 percent of each of the poll predictions.

4. For the newer treatments of Galton's Problem, see Burton and White (1991) for references; see also Dow (1991).

7

Coding Data

Collecting data for a cross-cultural study using secondary data should not be done before deriving the hypothesis or hypotheses to test, specifying measures and operational procedures for all the variables, pretesting, and specifying a sample of cases to study. This chapter discusses some additional issues to consider. These include:

- Coders: Who should collect the data? Should the same person collect the data and code the data? How many people should code each variable? Should the same person code the independent and dependent variables? Should the coders know the hypothesis to be tested?
- Which time and place are you focusing on?
- What should the code sheet look like?

CODERS

In any scientific study it is always better to have more than one individual code data. This is to minimize the possibility of bias affecting the results. As we discussed in chapter 5, measurement error is not likely to lead to a false conclusion, like confirming a hypothesis that is in fact false. Error (systematic or random) is more likely to lead to failure to confirm a hypothesis that is in fact true. Unfortunately, it is impossible to know what the "true" score is for any case, but we may be more confident that we have gotten the score right if two or more people agree on the score.

Usually cross-cultural researchers try to have more than one coder for each variable so that they can assess the degree of agreement or reliability between coders. Chapter 9 deals with how to measure reliability and what to do about disagreements between coders. The usual reason a researcher does not have more than one coder is lack of funding. A researcher may be willing to devote time to the project, but it is unlikely that someone else will do so for free unless it is part of a classroom assignment or the coding can be done for course credit (e.g., in an independent study course).

One way of saving time and minimizing the expense of a second coder is to have one person collect or copy the relevant ethnographic passages in ethnography so that the second coder does not have to read and skim a lot of material before making a coding assessment. The disadvantage of this method is that if the first coder misses some relevant material, the second coder won't see it either. Even though it is more time-consuming, it is probably better to have each coder browse through the material independently and then do the coding. That way you maximize the probability of finding information that may affect a coding decision, but it does take more time.

It is probably not necessary to have more than two well-trained coders. (Ideally, training should take place with a set of cases that are not used in the final study.) If there are disagreements about particular cases, those cases can be reviewed later by both coders or by a third coder.

Since the purpose of most cross-cultural research is to test a hypothesis to try to falsify a theory, it seems preferable to have at least one coder who does not know the hypothesis to be tested. Coders, however, are usually curious about what they are doing and why, so it may be difficult to really keep them in the dark about the hypotheses. Therefore, it is preferable for different coders to code the independent and the dependent variables. If the two variables are not described in the same passages, it is very unlikely that the coding on one variable could influence the coding on the other variable. If it is not possible to have two coders, it is much better for the person who knows the hypothesis to make different passes through the data, first coding one variable for the sample cases, then on a second pass coding the other variable. It is not likely, if you do one variable at a time, that you will remember how a case was coded on a variable previously coded. Coding each variable separately also has another advantage—it is easier to keep the operational definitions and the coding rules clear if you read for coding one variable at a time.

TIME AND PLACE FOCUS

In chapter 5, on minimizing error, we talked about the importance of adhering to a particular time and place focus for each case. If the researcher is using variables that were coded in another study, the time and place focus should match those of the previous study. To get a coder to read the material for the intended time and place, the researcher should specify in advance the appropriate ethnographies to read, or, if the coder is selecting material from the Human Relations Area Files (HRAF), the appropriate ethnographers or document numbers should be indicated on the code sheet. (A concordance [C. R. Ember 1992] published by HRAF matches documents in HRAF to the time and place foci of commonly used cross-cultural samples.)

If you wish to allow a coder to deviate from the intended time and place, coding instructions should clearly indicate whether or not such a deviation is allowed. If the investigator allows deviations, we recommend that each case be coded for the degree to which the time and place focus was adhered to. Like the data quality control codes, a separate code can be constructed for the degree to which the time and place focus is similar to or different from the intended focus. Then the researcher can test whether deviations from time and place foci affect the results. Deviant cases should show weaker results, assuming that results should generally be stronger if you have measured your variables for the same time and place for a given case.

FORM OF THE CODE SHEET

Nowadays, code sheets can be in paper or electronic form. We do not recommend entering coded data directly into a database or statistical program that does not allow sufficient room for notes and comments.

There are three major components in a code sheet. A fourth is optional.

1. Identifying information including:

- the name of the project
- the name of the case
- a unique identification number to be used in data entry
- a specified time focus with an indication of how much the coder can depart from that time
- a particular place focus, if applicable (not all ethnographers indicate what community they worked in)
- the date of coding (so that change over time in coding practice could be evaluated)
- the name of the coder.

2. Operational procedures for measuring the variable. We recommend rating each variable on a separate code sheet unless the variables are very close conceptually and the information pertaining to them almost always comes from the same place (e.g., frequency of corporal punishment and severity of corporal punishment may be two separate variables, but they are likely to be discussed together in the ethnography and could go on one coding sheet).

- the name of the variable
- the operational definition of the variable
- the scale scores that are to be used; an indication of whether or not a coder can use intermediate scores if the positions are ordinal or interval
- instructions regarding where to find the appropriate information; if coding is done using the Human Relations Area Files, the appropriate search strategy should be given—see appendix.

3. A place for indicating coding decisions and pertinent information.

- a clear place for entering the coding decision
- a place for entering relevant quotes and/or documents and page numbers that back up the coding decision
- a place to enter reasons for a decision if there are no explicit statements or no explicit quotes

4. (Optional) A data quality code for each variable and appropriate instructions (see discussion in chapter 5).

A CODING EXERCISE

Note: Don't look at the information in table 7.1 until after you do this exercise.

Box 7.1 shows coding instructions for the frequency of corporal punishment of children. Please read all the instructions carefully. After you read the material for each case, excerpted below, reread the coding instructions before you make a judgment. Normally, if you were the coder in a study of corporal punishment you would not just be given abstracts. Rather, you would be asked to read through all the relevant material, taking notes only on material that pertains to the intended time and place. Assume that all of that has been done already and use the coding instructions to rate the following passages.

Society Name _____ *   ID# _____ *

Time Focus or Time Range _____ *   Place Focus, if any _____ *

Appropriate Sources _____   *(Note: if you use other sources

than the ones selected prior to coding, note why you used them, e.g., that the

later source refers back to the focal time and place.)

Date of Coding _____   Coder Name _____

Note—these pieces of information should be filled in by the researcher prior to coding.

Variable Name: Frequency of Corporal Punishment of Children

Definition: Corporal punishment is the act of hitting, striking, wounding or bruising a minor child for the purpose of punishing, disciplining, or showing disapproval.

Operational Procedures:

a. Use the Human Relations Area Files and search for the subject (OCM) category 861 (the name of this category is "Techniques of Inculcation"). If there is explicit and comprehensive information on the society you are examining and in the particular sources noted above, it is not necessary to read further. If the information is not that clear or ample enough for a judgment, look through other child rearing categories in the 85s and 86s.

b. Note that corporal punishment does not have to be administered by a parent, but could be administered by any caretaker or onlooker. The focus of the rating should be on the period after infancy and before adolescence.

c. Ethnographers who pay more attention to child rearing will usually give examples, even examples of unusual cases. Be careful not to weight contrary examples more heavily just because they are given. An ethnographer paying cursory attention to child rearing might just say "Children are rarely hit." Another ethnographer may say the same thing and then give examples of the rare times they are hit. This doesn't mean that corporal punishment is more common in the latter case.

d. Rate on the following scale **(Note: Intermediate positions are allowed, e.g., 1.5, 2.5)**:

   1. ***Rarely or never.*** Rare could be in one of two senses—most families hardly ever use corporal punishment or corporal punishment is characteristic only of a rare family.
      - Do not infer the absence of corporal punishment from the absence of information on the subject of discipline or how children are treated. The ethnographer must describe alternative methods of discipline or how caretakers treat children in enough detail for you to judge that corporal punishment is rarely used.

Box 7.1. Sample Code Sheet (adapted from C. R. Ember and M. Ember, n.d.).

- Do not consider the supposed lightness of the hit or strike (severity of punishment will be rated separately).
- If the ethnographer only describes infancy and does not describe corporal punishment during that period, do not assume that it is lacking in subsequent stages unless there is explicit information on other stages.

2. **Frequent, but not typical.** Corporal punishment is used for some categories of misbehavior that occur fairly often, but it is not the usual method of discipline. There are many types of punishment (warning, scolding, etc.), so do not assume that the word "punishment" means corporal punishment.

3. **Typical.** Use this category if corporal punishment seems to be the usual mode of discipline for almost any kind of misbehavior. But do not infer that "punishment" means corporal punishment.

8. **Confusing or contradictory.** Do not use this category if you can make an intermediate score (e.g., 2.5), if you think it is either 2 or 3. If you can't decide between 1 and 3, code as confusing.

9. **Not enough information to make a judgment.**

Scale Score _____ *(Allowed scores 1, 1.5, 2, 2.5, 3, 8, or 9)*
Sources and page numbers relevant to decision

_____

_____

Attach relevant quotes or photocopies. Identify any attached pages with ID#, variable name, coder name, source, and page identification.

Box 7.1. Continued

Ojibwa (Chippewa):

Although reward and punishment, scolding, and frightening played a part in the training of many Chippewa children, no great emphasis was laid upon them. Every attempt was made to make children mind by speaking to them as occasion arose or by teaching them to do so at times of formal education.

The child was usually not given much praise; occasionally it was given a reward, such as maple sugar, a toy carved out of wood, or a doll of grass, for work well done.

Sensible parents, informants agreed, never ridiculed their children for failures. Children were scolded, but "too much scolding often made them worse." At times a child was frightened by some masked person; more often by expressions such as these: "The Sioux will get you." "You lazy old thing: you don't know anything, and you'll never have anything either." "The owl will put you in his ears!" "The owl will put you in his ears, and fly away with your little feet sticking out of his ears!". . . If children refused to go to sleep at night, mothers poked their heads out of wigwams and called the owl, say-ing "*Ko-ko-ko!* Now hear the owl!" (HRAF Source 13: Hilger, p. 58)

Rwala:

Until their seventh year both boys and girls remain with their mother, going to their father only for an occasional talk. If their mother is not divorced by their father, they live in the women's compartment and help with the lighter work. If they deserve it they are spanked with a stick, not only by their mother or father, but by the slaves both male and female. The Rwala believe that the rod origi-nated in Paradise, *al-'asa azharat min al-genna*, and that it also leads man back to it. . . . Boys learn to shoot before they are fourteen and take part in at least one raid before they are sixteen. At this period the father would not think of pun-ishing the disobedience of his son simply with a stick but uses a saber or a dag-ger instead. By cutting or stabbing them the father not merely punishes the boys but hardens them for their future life. In the opinion of the Bedouins the son who disobeys is guilty of rebellion, for which the proper punishment is the saber, *as-seif lemin 'asa'*. (HRAF Source 2: Musil, p. 255–56)

Ifugao:

From birth they [children] are accustomed to do as they please in every thing on account of the extremely bad education which they receive from parents, who, although they hate like death the least domination on the part of strangers, submit like slaves to the caprice and insolence of their children. . . . They do not whip or punish them as do the Christian natives. The lightest slap is not employed among the Ifugaos, and would be received very badly and criticised among the others if it should be observed at any time. The most that happens, especially with the women—the mothers—is to shout at them, when their caprices are too repugnant and prejudicial to the interests of the house, but they gain nothing by this, because if they (the children) are small they only weep harder, and if they are larger they pick up stones or lances, and attack their parents, driving them out of the house, to which they do not return until they see the children pacified and quiet. (HRAF Source 19: Villaverde et al. 1869–79, p. 245)

Tiv:

The most important social prohibitions early taught to children are that they must not ask other people for food and that they must not steal. Normally the issue seldom arises. Children visiting from other compounds should be offered food if there is any about . . . if a child, especially one over five years old, takes food too often, he is severely scolded and sometimes slapped, by his mother.

Children who do something wrong also have to face public ridicule. It is, indeed, the common Tiv method of bringing pressure to bear on any straying individual. . . . Children are very aware that theft is a very serious crime and is followed by serious consequences. Whenever a thief is caught, part of his punishment is being marched about before all the population of the compound, and all words "Look at the thief!" . . . Mothers hold up their children to watch and tell them, "See, this is what happens to a thief."

Disciplining a child should be left to his own parents. Even when disciplining is taken over by the compound head, because several households are involved, it is up to the child's own father to administer any physical punishment decided upon. . . . When two children are fighting each other, the closest adult pulls them apart and scolds both. If there is a parent within earshot, that adult yells, "Shan't I beat them?" and, without waiting for an answer, he may do so, lightly. Two women who are on good terms with each other both scold and slap the hands of each other's children. (HRAF Source 22: Bohannan and Bohannan, pp. 369–71)

Pawnee (Skidi):

The early training of the child was largely in the hands of the grandmothers, who took it upon themselves to give instruction in tribal and family ethics. They assumed the right to enforce their injunctions and commands by blows or by the use of the whip, and it is claimed that in former times, before the Skidi had been modified through contact with white men, the rearing of children was very strict and they were often scolded and severely punished by the father, mother, or grandparents. Aside from the deference young children were supposed to pay adults, they were taught to show respect for their parents by not molesting them, to remain silent when older people were talking, to refrain from approaching too closely the altar in the earth lodge, and carefully to avoid making a disturbance about the scenes of ceremonies. During this period an older sister might assist in correcting the child. As a boy grew older he was given technical instruction by his grandfathers in the making of bows and arrows, in the playing of games, etc. Girls were taught by their grandmothers to prepare food, to dress hides, and to do the work which fell to the lot of women. This early training was often supplemented by the telling of myths containing some moral precept. For example, the child was told not to steal, the point being especially illustrated by the tale of the boy who stole his sister's seed corn, and, because he grew angry for being scolded, turned into an eagle. (HRAF Source 5: Dorsey and Murie, p. 94)

Saami (Skolt):

During the field work period there was ample opportunity to observe children making noise and getting into mischief in Skolt homes. A great many activities which would have called for positive action if in an average American home passed unnoticed or with only minor action in the Skolt households. . . . Considerable patience is generally exercised by Skolt parents in ignoring noise and mischief, though coaxing, distracting, and other means are used to keep children under some minimum of restraint while visitors

Table 7.1. Coding Decisions

Culture	Freq. of Corp. Punish. (CRE)	Freq. of Corp. Punish. (ME)	Notes by CRE
Ojibwa	1	1	Although it is not said that corporal punishment is rare, there is discussion of other techniques of punishment—scolding and frightening are mentioned with no mention made of corporal punishment. Infer rare.
Rwala	3	3	Although the phrase "If they deserve it, they are spanked with a stick" is somewhat ambiguous (it could mean if they are very naughty or it could mean that whenever they are bad they are hit), the rest of the paragraph strongly suggests that corporal punishment is the method of choice.
Ifugao	1	1	Even though the author (a missionary) appears biased in calling the Ifugao "bad parents" because they do not punish their children as Christians would, the description suggests that the author paid sufficient attention to child rearing to suggest that the description is accurate.
Tiv	2	2	Scolding is mentioned first in paragraph 1 discussed in the text; slapping is said to occur "sometimes." Ridicule is mentioned as "the common Tiv method." Since corporal punishment is clearly employed, score 2 seems the appropriate choice.
Pawnee	2.5	2	Since grandmothers have the right to enforce their commands by blows or use of a whip, it is clear that corporal punishment is employed. That sentence, however, does not indicate frequency. The phrase "often scolded and severely punished by the father, mother, or grandparents" suggests (in view of the fact that blows and whipping are mentioned) that both techniques are used frequently.
Saami	1.5	2	The ethnographer indicates that the Saami are relatively permissive about most childhood misbehavior except for aggression for which corporal punishment is used. That is why CRE scored them 1.5. However, the phrase "spanking and scolding occur for a wide variety of reasons" suggested to ME that corporal punishment was frequent.

are in the house. Some examples from field notes will illustrate this aspect of training:

Continued crying and whining may also be handled by scaring; the threat that is introduced always refers to someone or something outside the household group. Older women appear to be especially fond of coaxing a child into more restrained behavior by saying . . . That man (the anthropologist) will take you away in his big pack. . . . Perhaps we're going to have to give you away to this . . . uncle . . . if you can't stop crying.

All the disciplining discussed so far may be described as mild, permissive, and unhurried. Spanking has been mentioned in connection with toilet training (though apparently not often used), and spankings and scoldings occur for wide varieties of other reasons, but *strong* disciplining, including spanking, is particularly associated with control of aggression—fighting and teasing among siblings. Peaceful interaction, particularly within the household, is so highly valued among the Skolts that strong disciplinary measures are felt to be necessary to curb aggression, so it is in connection with fighting and teasing that getting spanked is most frequently remembered by Skolts. (HRAF Source 20: Pelto, pp. 98 and 100)

Record your scores on a separate piece of paper for each culture. After you have finished, compare your scores with the ones we have made in table 7.1.

Remember that coding decisions always depend somewhat on interpretations, so your answers may or may not be exactly the same as ours. And we ourselves disagreed slightly (by half a point) on two of the cases—Saami and Pawnee. If you have a serious disagreement with our codings, reread the coding rules and the passages to be sure that there is a real disagreement. As we discuss in more detail in chapter 9 on reliability, a researcher can deal with disagreements in various ways, each with advantages and disadvantages. As we shall see, final coding scores can be summed, averaged, or resolved, or cases with serious disagreements can be dropped. Whatever method is chosen, coding sheets and reasons for decisions should be preserved for later analysis.

8

Statistical Analysis

While this chapter does not presuppose sophistication in statistical analysis, and is not designed to substitute for formal training, we do try to summarize *why* statistical analysis is necessary for testing hypotheses cross-culturally. And we do discuss the major tools that you will need to understand research that includes statistical results, tables, and figures. Statistics cannot really be taught in one chapter of a book, but we try.

Descriptive statistics and inferential statistics have very different purposes. **Descriptive statistics** are used to summarize data to make them comprehensible. **Inferential statistics** allow researchers to generalize their sample results to a larger universe, assuming that the sampling is unbiased and the research design is appropriate. Let us first turn to some basic ways of summarizing data.

DESCRIPTIVE STATISTICS

Consider the example of a classroom test taken by 131 students. One student asks how the class did in general. Suppose the professor were to hand out a piece of paper with 131 numbers on it ordered in the sequence in which the individual papers were graded. Such a list would be hardly comprehensible. To be sure, the list would answer the question of how the class performed, but it doesn't answer the question in any clear way. Probably the real intent of the student's question was to find out how he or she did compared to everyone else. Most professors therefore usually put a frequency distribution on the board, showing how often a group of scores occurred. A frequency distribution provides a count of the number of people who got a particular score or one of a group of scores (A, B, C, etc., or a numerical range). When there are many possible scores, such as on a test with a hundred points, the professor could group the scores as shown in table 8.1. Looking down the frequency column tells you at a glance that more people got scores between 70 and 79 than any other range of scores. An alternative is to give percentages (see the "Percentage" column in table 8.1), which are just the frequency counts divided by the number of cases and multiplied by 100. A more graphic way of showing the information would be to show the frequency distribution as a bar chart as shown in figure 8.1. The vertical axis shows the frequency or number of people in each group of scores on the horizontal axis.

A measure of **central tendency** summarizes the data more succinctly. Such a measure conveys the center of the distribution with one number. We are very used to one measure of central tendency—what we call the *average* (the **mean** in the language of statistics). We are used to computing averages. You just add up all the scores and divide by the number of cases. For the data shown in table 8.1 and figure 8.1, the average score is 78.63. There are two other common measures of central tendency—the **median** and the **mode**. The *median* score is that number below and above which 50 percent of the scores fall. In other words, if we rank-order the scores, the median would be the score of the middle case. If we rank-order the actual grades behind the grouped scores in table 8.1, the median score is 79. The *mode* is the score with the highest frequency. If there are many different scores, the test score with the highest frequency doesn't make much sense to compute. But if we group the scores as shown in table 8.1 and figure 8.1, the modal group (with 53 scores) is the 70–79 range.

In the grade example just discussed, the mean, median, and grouped mode are almost identical. Why would we use one measure of central tendency over another to describe the center? The answer is that in most roughly symmetrical distributions, the measure of central tendency doesn't much matter. But it matters a lot if the distribution is skewed or not balanced, as the following example shows.

Let us suppose that we are interested in the typical income in three different communities. Table 8.2 shows the income of nine households in each community. (We normally would look at more households, but we are only looking at nine here to make the point easier to see.) Suppose we compute the mean (average) and the median scores for each community (see table 8.2). Let's look at the mean scores first. If we look only at the mean scores, we might mistakenly infer that the "typical" household in Community 1 has a higher income (mean = $34,167) than the "typical" household in Community 2 (mean = $14,222). So why do the median

Table 8.1.   Summary of Classroom Grades (Frequency Distribution and Percentages)

Scores	Frequency	Percentage
90–100	20	15.3
80–89	42	32.1
70–79	53	40.5
60–69	11	8.4
< 60	5	3.8
Total	**131**	**100.0**

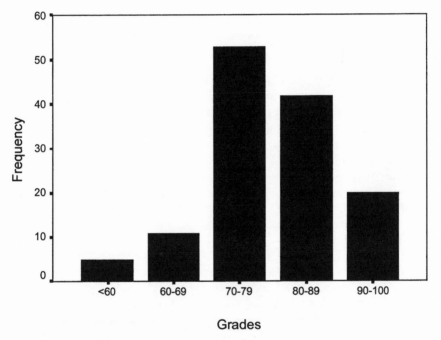

Figure 8.1.   Bar Graph of Grade Distribution.

scores not suggest the same kind of difference? The median scores suggest that the "typical" household in Community 1 makes $12,500. The two measures of central tendency are quite different (about $24,000 different)!

It is important to recognize then that the three measures of central tendency may work differently in different circumstances. If we look at the actual numbers again, we notice that one household in Community 1 (the last row in the Community 1 column) has an income well beyond any other household in the community. That household earns $200,000, which is at least $180,000 more than the others; none of the others earns more

Table 8.2. Yearly Income in Nine Households in Each of Three Communities

Community 1	Community 2	Community 3
$ 11,000	$ 9,000	$ 7,700
12,500	14,000	6,900
14,000	13,000	8,500
19,500	19,000	7,500
20,000	14,500	23,000
9,000	12,500	57,000
10,000	10,000	67,000
11,500	16,000	59,000
200,000	20,000	55,000
Mean $34,167	Mean $14,222	Mean $32,400
Median $12,500	Median $14,000	Median $23,000

than $20,000. The mean is high for Community 1 because when you compute a sum with one or a few very extreme numbers, the sum is heavily influenced by those numbers. The mean is analogous to the center of gravity (Senter 1969: 63–66). We all have had the experience of balancing on a seesaw with a friend about our size. What if we try to balance with a much heavier older child or a parent? We get pushed way up in the air. The only way to balance the seesaw is for the bigger person to move close to the balance point. (The lighter person could hardly move back!) If we think of the mean as being at the center of gravity or the point of balance, the mean will be influenced by a very skewed distribution that pulls it toward the extreme score(s) on one end. Notice that the median, which is the "middle" case, is not influenced by an extreme score. With regard to Community 1, four households have more income than $12,500 ($14,000, 19,500, 20,000 and 200,000) and four households have less. It doesn't matter whether the highest number is $200,000 or $21,000—the median remains the same. So, with a very skewed distribution, the median may give a better indication of where the center is. There is one circumstance where the median (as well as the mean) may be misleading. That instance is where there are few or no cases in the middle. Look at figure 8.2, which shows the distribution of income in Community 3, grouped into $5,000 ranges (from the data in table 8.2). The median for income in Community 3 is $23,000, but most households have either much lower income or much higher income. In this instance, we would be better off describing the shape of the distribution. This kind of distribution would be called bimodal; there are four households with very low incomes ($5,000-$9,999) and an equal number of households with incomes above $45,000. A researcher with a bimodal distribution would describe it more accurately in terms of modes than in terms of the mean or median. (Even distributions

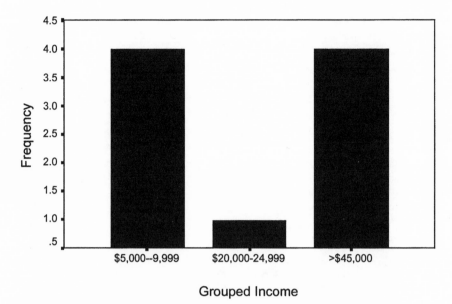

Grouped Income

Figure 8.2.   Distribution of Income in Community 3.

that did not have exactly equal modes would still be discussed as bimodal if the pattern looked similar to that shown in figure 8.2).

So far the scales we have summarized are interval and ratio scales. Recall that we said in chapter 4 that nominal scales only convey difference and ordinal scales only convey order. Means and median scores are best reserved for interval and ratio scales. If you wish to summarize nominal scores or grouped ordinal scores for a set of cases, it is best to use frequencies or percentage summaries. A modal score can also be given for the scale score with the highest frequency.

One other common kind of descriptive statistic is a *measure of variability*. This kind of measure helps us understand how much the scores are spread out. Two classes can have average scores of 75 on a test. But in one class grades range from 20 to 100, while in the other class the grades range from 69 to 81. What we want is a measure conveying that the variability is wide in one class, but narrow in the other. The simplest measure of variability is a **range**. You can describe the grades in the first class as having a mean of 75 with a range of 80 points (100 – 20); the second class as having a mean of 75 with a range of 12 points (81 – 69). The main trouble with a range is that it is defined solely by the highest and lowest scores. If almost every score is clustered in the middle except for one or a few, the range would suggest a lot more average variability than exists. A better measure of variability is to use the distance of every single score from the center and calculate some kind of average distance from the center. The most common such measures in statistics are the **variance** and the **standard deviation**. The variance is calculated as follows. The mean is subtracted from every score and the difference is squared. Then the squared distances are summed and the total is divided by the number of cases.[1] The result is the *variance*. If you take the square root of this number, you have the *standard deviation*. Why are the distances squared? Couldn't you just sum the distances? No, because if you subtract the mean from every score, some numbers will be positive and some will be negative; and if you sum them, they will cancel each other out. Squaring is one way to get rid of negative numbers before you sum them. To transform the variance to the original scale, you need to take the square root of the variance. Let's look again at the income variability of Communities 1, 2 and 3, using the standard deviation. First look at table 8.2. Intuitively, Community 2 looks like it has the tightest cluster of income. Community 3 is pretty variable because four households make less than $9,000 and four make at least $55,000. Community 1 is more variable because one household (with $200,000) is far different from the others. Now let us compare the standard deviations for the three:

Standard Deviation

Community 1	62,310.21
Community 2	3,692.15
Community 3	38,692.14

The standard deviations convey the degree of variability we intuited. Community 2 has the least variability, Community 3 the next, and Community 1 has the most.

There is one other kind of descriptive statistic that is important—summarizing how strongly variables are related to one another. Because such summaries are usually calculated in the context of inferring a result to a larger universe of cases, we discuss them in the next section.

INFERENTIAL STATISTICS

When researchers look at a sample of cases, they usually are not just looking to describe what they observe. They usually want to be able to generalize to a wider set of cases. When political pollsters ask a sample of individuals whom they will vote for, they usually are not content to say that Politician X wins in this sample. They are interested in predicting how all the voters will vote in the election; they want to be able to predict the winner in the election. Pollsters know that they cannot predict exactly, but they want to predict correctly within a small margin of error. When researchers are looking for a vaccine to prevent a deadly disease, they have to do clinical trials to see if the vaccinated are more likely to resist the disease than the unvaccinated, and then they can recommend use of the vaccine in the larger population. When we ask whether hunter-gatherers are more peaceful than agriculturalists, we are asking about the situation generally; we don't just mean among the cases we are looking at.

While we never can know for sure what is true in the larger set of cases, because it would be too time-consuming or expensive to find out, most inferential statistical techniques rest on a few very simple principles:

- It is assumed that the sample you have chosen is unbiased. The best way to achieve that is to select the sample cases randomly from the larger universe of cases you wish to generalize to (this is why sampling strategies are so important).
- A statistical "test of significance" will evaluate how likely it is that your result (or a better result) is due solely to chance. This is like playing devil's advocate. The reasoning goes like this. Let's pretend there is no difference or no relationship. What is the probability of getting the results you got (and better results) by accident? The lower the chance, the more we can believe that the result from the sample is correct.

These principles are simple. But learning statistics is complicated because different kinds of tests make different assumptions about the data, and different types of measures require different types of tests. While computer programs make computations easy, they do not readily tell you whether a particular type of test is appropriate. If you give numbers for your variables to your computer, it will compute anything, even if it is not appropriate.

Tests about Relationships between Two Nominal Variables

In chapter 1, we introduced the notion of contingency tables, which we discussed further in chapter 5. Such tables are useful for displaying how the sample cases are distributed in a cross-tabulation of the two nominal or categorical variables. Contingency tables may also be used to look at a relationship between two ordinal variables (that convey more or less of some quality or quantity), if there aren't more than five or so scale points on each variable. And contingency tables can be used to examine an association between one nominal and one ordinal variable. The simplest contingency table is referred to as a "2 by 2" table (two rows and two columns). If there were a perfect relationship between the two dichotomous variables, we would expect all the cases to fall into the two cells on one diagonal, as in the first table shown in box 8.1.

Displaying a contingency table is not enough. We can look at the first table in box 8.1 and say that the relationship looks perfect because all the cases are on the diagonal. But in this table there are only four cases and we might suspect that the result could be due to chance. Box 8.1 takes you through the steps of computing the probability that this "perfect" result is due to chance.

We now have our probability; it is $p = .167$. So is our hypothesis supported? To decide whether we accept or reject our hypothesis, we have to have a decision rule as to whether we will accept our hypothesis or not. It is best to set this rule *before* conducting your test. There is no right or wrong p-value. If it is a matter of life and death where you can't afford to be wrong, you might want to see a very low chance of an accidental association. However, when you make it harder to be wrong, you also make it harder to find associations that are probably true. Most social scientists accept the convention that if the probability of the result occurring by chance is *less than or equal to .05*, we can accept the hypothesis. If the p-value is .05 or lower, we say that the association is **statistically significant**. If the p-value is greater than .05, most researchers would reject the hypothesis. Given this convention about what to conclude from p-values, we would say that the relationship displayed near the top of box 8.1 is not significant, because the p-value is *higher* than .05. Instead of writing the exact probability under our table we would probably write:

$$p > .05, \text{ one tail, by Fisher's Exact Test}$$

However, keep in mind that the example we are considering involves only four cases. Realistically, we would not test this hypothesis with four cases because it is not possible to get a statistically significant result with only four sample cases in a contingency table. The minimum number of cases that might provide a significant result is six, but the result has to be perfect. (If the table had been 3, 0, 0, 3, the p-value would have been .05 because there are twenty possible ways the six cases could be distributed and only one way the 3, 0, 0, 3 table could occur; hence the p-value would be 1 divided by 20 or .05.) If we really wanted to give this hypothesis a chance, we would probably choose a random sample of at least twenty cases, because there are almost always exceptions (cases that fall into the unpredicted cells because of measurement error, cultural lag, other causes, etc.). There are formulas and tables for looking up exact probabilities according to Fisher's Exact Test for 2 by 2 tables with up to fifty cases. But most researchers would use the **chi-square test** for the significance of a contingency table that contains more than twenty or thirty cases. This is

To make it easy to compute the probability of a particular result, we are deliberately going to use a very small sample. Suppose we randomly draw two hunting-gathering societies and two agricultural societies. Our hypothesis is that the hunter-gatherers will tend to lack permanent settlements. *The alternative hypothesis, which the statistical test evaluates, is that there is no relationship between hunting-gathering and lack of permanent settlements.* Fisher's Exact Test computes the probability that our observed result is due to chance.

First, look at the result displayed immediately below. At first glance, the result looks perfect. Look at the hunter-gatherer row. Two of the two hunter-gatherer cases lack permanent settlements. And in the agricultural row, two of the two agricultural cases have permanent settlements. There are no exceptions.

	No Permanent Settlements	Permanent Settlements	Total
HG	2	0	**2**
Agric	0	2	**2**
Total	**2**	**2**	**4**

But is this result something we can trust, or is it due to chance? Here's where we can compute the chance of this result or a better one (in this case there is no better one) occurring by chance and chance alone. We see how many different ways the cases could fall by chance. There is only one constraint in this test. We must keep the totals the same. The totals, called the **marginals**, are bolded. In other words, we must have two cases fall in the hunter-gatherer row, two in the agricultural row, and two cases in each column.

Let us label the two hunter-gatherer cases "A" and "B" and the two agricultural cases "C" and "D." With the marginal constraints above, how many ways could the cases fall?

The table below shows each of the possible tables on the left (in bold). To the immediate right of each table are the possible combinations of A, B, C, and D that can make up this combination. Notice that for the perfect table we saw above, there is only one way the table can occur. But for the table below (1,1,1,1), with one case in each cell, there are four different ways the cases could be distributed. The last table, which is directly opposite to the hypothesis expected, could only occur in one way.

Box 8.1. Computing Exact Probabilities (Fisher's Exact Test)

2	0	AB		
0	2		CD	1

1	1	A	B	
1	1	C	D	
		A	B	
		D	C	
		B	A	
		C	D	4
		B	A	
		D	C	

0	2		AB	
2	0	CD		1

———
6

So, to return to the original question, what is the probability that the table we got at the very top of this box would occur by chance and chance alone? Since there are a total of six ways that these four cases could distribute themselves (add up all the A, B, C, D tables), the probability of table occurring by chance is 1 out of 6 or .167. We would write the following phrase under our observed table:

p = .167, one tail, by Fisher's Exact Test

What the phrase means is: The probability of this strong a result or a stronger result occurring by chance in this direction (which is what "one tail" means) is 1 out of 6 or about 17 times out of a hundred. The method of computation is Fisher's Exact Test. (For larger samples, you can use a formula or look up the exact probability in a published table.)

Notice that when we figured out the various combinations, there were two perfect tables—the top and the bottom ones. If we started out with a hypothesis that did not predict a direction, that is, "Permanence of settlements is related to type of subsistence (hunting-gathering versus agriculture)," the appropriate probability would be to add up the chances of all possible outcomes. So, we would add the probabilities .167 and .167 for the two directions. Then we would say p = .33, two tails, by Fisher's Exact Test.

Box 8.1. Continued

assuming that the chance-expected values (the values that would occur with no relationship) are 5 or more in each cell. Providing the expected values are large enough, chi-square tests can be calculated also when contingency tables are larger than 2 by 2.

Sometimes we want to know more than whether two variables are probably associated. We want to know how *strongly* they are associated. Usually we are looking for strong predictors because only they together would account for most of the cases. So, for example, if we want to understand why people in some societies go to war more often than people in other societies, we would expect a presumably causal variable to predict many cases, not just a few. Let's look now at the top two rows of table 8.3. In each row a perfect table is displayed on the left and a "nothing" table is displayed on the right. The difference between the top row and the bottom row is only in the number of cases in each table, 100 in the top row and 20 in the bottom row. Since the number of cases in the top row is 100, we use a chi-square test to evaluate the statistical significance of a result. (Consult a statistics book for the formula for computing chi-square and a table in which to look up the p-values for different values of chi-square. You will also need to know the degrees of freedom (df) in a table. A 2 x 2 table has 1 degree of freedom because given the row and column totals, once you know the number in *one* cell, you can calculate all the other cell values.) It is important to compute the test of significance first because the strength of an association is not relevant if the relationship is likely to be due to chance.

Notice that the first four left tables in the top row of table 8.3 can be described as statistically significant because the chi-square (χ^2) test gives associated p-values of less than or equal to .05. The first three tables are even more significant since they would be likely to occur by chance less than 1 time out of 1,000.

We can intuit that the table on the left shows a strong relationship because there are no exceptions—all the cases are on one of the diagonals. What we are looking for is a measure of association that will give a high score to the table on the left and a "zero relationship" score to the table on the extreme right. There are several measures of association for 2 by 2 tables. The different measures are usually based on different assumptions and they have different mathematical properties (so you cannot compare one measure of association with another). The most important thing to realize is that measures of association usually give scores (coefficients) that range between ±1.00 and .00. A coefficient of −1.00 means that the association is perfectly negative, that one variable goes up as the other goes down; a +1.00 coefficient means that one variable goes up as the other goes up. The direction is meaningful only when the pair of categories on each variable can be ordered (e.g., present versus absent, high versus low).

Table 8.3. Strength of Association (Phi) and Tests of Significance

50	0
0	50

phi = 1.00

$\chi^2 = 100$; df = 1, p <.001

45	5
5	45

phi = .80

$\chi^2 = 64$; df = 1, p<.001

35	15
15	35

phi = .40

$\chi^2 = 16$; df = 1, p <.001

30	20
20	30

phi = .20

$\chi^2 = 4$; df = 1, p <.05

25	25
25	25

phi = 0.00

$\chi^2 = 0.00$; df = 1, n.s.*

10	0
0	10

phi = 1.00

p <.01, two tails by Fisher's Exact Test

9	1
1	9

phi = .80

p <.01, two tails by Fisher's Exact Test

7	3
3	7

phi = .40

n.s.* (p >.05) by Fisher's Exact Test

6	4
4	6

phi = .20

n.s.* (p >.05) by Fisher's Exact Test

5	5
5	5

phi = 0.00

n.s.* (p >.05) by Fisher's Exact Test

*Not significant.

The phi (φ) coefficient is a commonly used measure of association for 2 by 2 tables. As you can see across the top row of table 8.3, the phi coefficients show that the strength of the relationship is weaker as you go from left to right. Notice that the tables in the second row have exactly the same proportion of cases on the diagonal as the top row tables. Not surprisingly, the phi coefficients are the same in the second row. However, only the two left-hand tables are statistically significant! We used Fisher's Exact Test because the number of cases is relatively small, but we could have used chi-square since the expected value in each cell is at least 5. This tells us that we cannot rely on the measure of association to draw an inference about statistical significance. We need to do the test of significance first.

While some might infer that it is better not to have a small sample because it is harder to get significant results, we would argue that it depends upon what you are looking to accomplish. If you are looking for strong predictors, a small sample may be advantageous. First, it is less work to code the cases for a small sample. Second, only strong associations will be significant.

One drawback of the phi coefficient is that it will only go to 1.00 (or –1.00) with a symmetrical relationship. For example, in table 8.4, the totals for the rows do not match the totals for the columns and the maximum phi coefficient possible is .67.

This may be fine for some purposes. After all, you may expect there to be exceptions, even with a strong relationship, and therefore you cannot expect the coefficient of association to be 1.00. But consider that each of the following theoretical models will produce different kinds of tables:

1. X is the only cause of Y (X is necessary and sufficient).
2. X is a sufficient cause of Y (that is, when X is present, Y is present; however, Y may have other causes and therefore Y may be present when X is absent).
3. X is a necessary cause of Y (that is, when X is absent, Y will be absent; however some additional factor is necessary for Y).

Table 8.4. Contingency Table with Unequal Column and Row Totals

Variable X	Variable Y		
	Present	*Absent*	*Total*
Present	40	0	40
Absent	20	40	60
Total	60	40	100

phi = .67

Notice that table 8.4 is more consistent with model 2 than with models 1 and 3. If Y has more than one cause, then we would expect exceptions to the table in one particular cell (when X is absent, Y may be present). Those exceptions do not mean that X and Y are not related in a causal way. If X were a necessary cause of Y, but not a sufficient cause, as model 3 suggests, we would expect a zero cell when X is absent and Y is present.

The point is that the statistical measure used should be consistent with the theoretical model you expect to apply. If you do not expect that X is the only cause of Y, you may wish to choose a coefficient of association that goes to 1.00 with just one zero cell. In a 2 by 2 table, the gamma coefficient of association (which can be used for an ordinal by ordinal association) may be a better choice than the phi coefficient if you want the coefficient to go to 1 when there is one zero cell.

Some other coefficients for contingency tables are:

- Lambda (based on how well you can predict Y from X, X from Y— the two coefficients may not be the same)
- Uncertainty Coefficient (based on how much uncertainty about one variable is reduced by knowing the other)

Table 8.5 summarizes the appropriate statistics for different types of variables.

Statistical Inference about Differences between Two Groups

Often a research question asks about differences between two samples or groups. Do males exhibit more aggression than females? Is one population taller than another? Do hunter-gatherers have lower population densities than agriculturalists? In all these questions, we have two nominal groups to compare. However, in contrast to using a contingency table that is most appropriate for the intersection between one nominal scale and another, the three questions above allow for the possibility of measuring the other variable on an interval or ratio scale. For example, you can compare the number of aggressive acts (in a particular period of time) in two groups of children, you can compare the average adult heights in two human populations, or you can compare the population densities of a sample of hunter-gatherers and a sample of agriculturalists.

Assuming that you find a difference in means between the two groups and that certain assumptions are met (see below), the most commonly used statistic to test the significance of the difference between means is the *t-test for independent samples* (each of the two groups consists of different individuals). As in most other statistical tests, the t-test evaluates statistical significance against the hypothesis that there is no difference between the groups.

Table 8.5. Type of Statistical Analysis for the Relationship between Two Variables*

	Nominal—Two Categories	Nominal—Three or More Categories	Ordinal	Interval
Nominal—Two Categories	Tests of Significance • Fisher's Exact Test • Chi-square Measures of Associaton: • Phi • Yule's Q (Gamma) • Lambda • Uncertainty Coefficient	Tests of Significance: • Chi-square Measures of Association: • Phi (but can get larger than 1.00) • Cramer's V • Lambda • Uncertainty Coefficient	Tests of Significance: • Mann-Whitney U • Kolmogorov-Smirnov Z	Tests of Significance: • t-Test Measure of Association: • point biserial r
Nominal—Three or More Categories		Tests of Significance: • Chi-square Measures of Association: • Phi (but can get larger than 1.00) • Cramer's V • Lambda • Uncertainty Coefficient	Tests of Significance: • Kruskal-Wallis analysis of variance	Tests of Significance: • Analysis of Variance
Ordinal			Measures of Association: • Spearman's rho** • Kendall's tau** • Gamma**	Treat as ordinal by ordinal
Interval or Ratio				Measures of Association: • Pearson's r (for linear relationships)** Tests of Fit for Different Curves

*The statistical tests included do not exhaust all of those available.
**Can all be tested for significance.

In other words, the t-test asks how likely is it that a difference of magnitude X (or a bigger difference) could occur by chance if the larger populations from which the samples are drawn actually have the same mean scores.

An example of data that would be appropriate for a t-test is the hypothetical comparison of height (in inches) in adult males compared with adult females shown in table 8.6.

If we perform a t-test for independent samples, we get the following results:

$$t = 2.361, df = 16, p = .03, \text{two tails}$$

Once again, the p-value tells us the likelihood that this difference is due to chance and chance alone. Since the p-value is less than .05, the conventional level of significance, we can reject the hypothesis of no difference and accept the hypothesis that there is a significant difference in height between males and females. The p-value is given as two-tailed, which means that we have allowed for the possibility of a difference in height in either direction (males taller than females, females taller than males). The df (degree of freedom) is the total number of cases (18) minus the number of groups (2).

Assumptions of the t-test:

1. The data are measured on interval or ratio scales.
2. The populations have "normal" distributions on the measured variables. This means that the frequency distributions for the variables in both populations are roughly bell-shaped. The modal height is at the center and the curve slopes down symmetrically with very few cases at the extremes.
3. The variances (or the standard deviations) for the two populations are roughly the same.
4. The cases were randomly selected from their respective populations.

Table 8.6.   A Hypothetical Comparison of Height (in Inches) in a Sample of Adult Males Compared with Adult Females

Females	Males
66	69
72	65
60	75
65	74
62	66
71	68
63	71
64	67
65	70
mean = 65.33	mean = 69.44

The t-test is relatively robust; it can tolerate some violation of its assumptions. But you could use tests that do not require the same assumptions. Because the t-test assumes certain characteristics or parameters (assumptions 2 and 3 above) about the populations the samples come from, the t-test is called a *parametric* test. **Parametric tests** make certain assumptions about the underlying distributions, such as that the distribution is normally distributed. **Nonparametric tests**, sometimes called "distribution-free" tests (Siegel 1956: 19), do not require parametric assumptions about the data.

Nonparametric tests to evaluate the difference between two groups are of course particularly useful if you have ordinal (rank-order) rather than interval measures. For example, in the height example above, if we did not have measurements by ruler, we could line the persons up by size and assign the shortest person the lowest rank (1) and the tallest person the highest rank (18). One nonparametric test of difference between two groups, called the *Mann-Whitney U test*, evaluates the significance of the difference between one group's average rank and the other group's average rank. This test is analogous to the t-test, but makes no assumptions about the underlying distributions. If we perform a Mann-Whitney U test on the same data used in the t-test above, we find that the average rank of the males is 12.22 and the average rank of the females is 6.78. The Mann-Whitney U is 16 and $p < .02$, two tails. In this example, the Mann-Whitney U test gives a p-value that is similar to the p-value given by the t-test, and this is generally true if we compare the outcomes of the two tests on the same data (Siegel 1956: 126). That is, the Mann-Whitney U test can detect significant differences between two groups just about as well as the t-test, without having to make parametric assumptions. Another nonparametric test for the significance of the difference between independent groups is the *Kolmogorov-Smirnov* test (Siegel 1956: 127ff.).

Statistical Inferences about Differences among Three or More Groups

Suppose you want to compare more than two nominal groups on an interval variable. Perhaps you want to compare three or four populations on height, or compare population densities of hunter-gatherers, pastoralists, horticulturalists, and intensive agriculturalists.

A parametric test can be used to test whether the means of more than two groups are significantly different. (If they are, we can say that the differences in means are unlikely to be due to chance.) This test is called a *one-way analysis of variance (ANOVA)*.[2] But what if the parametric assumptions cannot be met? Fortunately, there is also a nonparametric equivalent called the *Kruskal-Wallis one-way analysis of variance*. Like the Mann-Whitney U test, the Kruskal-Wallis test uses rank-ordered scores.

This test is also almost as powerful as the parametric analysis of variance (Siegel 1956).

With three or more groups the inferential statistics and the associated p-values only tell you whether or not the differences in the sets of scores are unlikely to be due to chance. However, you cannot infer without further testing where the difference lies. Suppose you have three groups, A, B, and C. Perhaps all three groups are significantly different from each other, but it is possible that only one group is different from the others. And, if one is different, it could be A, B, or C that is different from the others. Most computer programs have special routines for testing the difference between any pair of groups after the overall analysis of variance is performed.

Measures of Association and Tests of Significance for Interval and Ordinal Variables

All the associations (or differences) we have discussed so far involve at least one nominal variable. Now we turn to relationships with more continuous scales—interval or ratio scales, or ordinal scales with many ranks.

Interval Variables

To examine the relationship between two interval scales, it is important first to plot the cases on a graph with an X and a Y axis and look at the scatter plot of points. This is good to do first because the relationship when plotted may not look linear. If it does, you measure the strength of the association in the usual way (i.e., by using *Pearson's r*); if the relationship looks curvilinear, you should use another, more appropriate measure (e.g., *eta*) for the strength of the relationship. (See any statistics text for information about these measures.) The convention is to put the dependent variable on the Y axis and the independent variable on the X axis. Bergmann's Rule (C. R. Ember and M. Ember 1999: 116) suggests that human populations living in colder climates have more body mass (weight). The reasoning is that it is more adaptive in cold climates to have more body mass, because the body conserves heat better the more mass it has. To test this directional hypothesis, Roberts (1953) conducted a cross-cultural comparison and found support for Bergmann's Rule. We don't show his data here, but let us imagine that a plot of temperature and weight (one point for each population) would look something like the plot shown in figure 8.3. How would we describe this relationship? We could say that, in general, colder temperatures are associated with more weight, but we could also describe the relationship in statistical terms. If the relationship looks roughly linear, as this one does, linear regression is a method for getting a straight line that best fits a set of points. It is important to try linear regression only when the relationship looks roughly linear.[3] The most common method used is called "least squares." Basically we arrive at a straight line that minimizes the squared vertical deviations of all the points from the line.[4] Most computers do such computations in a very short time. If we do the least squares computation for X as a function of Y in our hypothetical data set (shown in figure 8.3), we get the line plotted in figure 8.4. If we want to predict Y (average weight) from X (average temperature), we can use the formula for the line or the line itself to say what the weight would be if the average temperature were 45° Fahrenheit.

But the line or the formula for the line doesn't tell us how strong the linear relationship is. (A line of best fit can be calculated for any set of points, no matter how much the points deviate from the line.) Pearson's r is a measure of the strength of a linear relationship. Just as with most other coefficients of association, Pearson's r is 0.00 if there is no linear relationship and ±1.00 if all the points fall exactly on the line. (Remember that a minus sign would mean that as one variable goes up, the other goes down; a plus sign would mean that one variable goes up as the other goes up.) In our hypothetical data set, the r is –.949. (As average temperature increases, average weight decreases.) The coefficient is so strong (close to –1.00) because the points are not far off the line.

So far, everything we have described about linear regression is *descriptive*. That is, we have just described how you can get a formula for the best linear fit and a measure of the degree to which the points fall on a straight line. Neither of these things tells us whether the linear-looking relationship might be due to chance and chance alone. Remember that a best-fitting straight line can be drawn for any set of points, even one that does not look linear!

It is important then to test the significance of your measure of association. What is evaluated is the probability that the obtained coefficient (or a stronger one) could be due to chance if the true linear relationship were zero. In our example, the r could be positive or negative, but we would look for the one-tailed significance because the direction of the relationship was predicted. The p-value for our hypothetical data set is <.0005, one tail. This means that the likelihood of there being no negative linear relationship is less than 5 times in 10,000.

What if the relationship is not linear? Figure 8.5 shows an example of a nonlinear relationship. If we didn't plot our data but just asked for a Pearson's r, we would have gotten an r of 0.00 because the line of best fit in figure 8.5 is flat. (A flat line means that the best predictor of Y for each value of X is the mean of Y.) If the variation on X doesn't help us predict the variation on Y any better than using the mean of Y, there is no relationship between X and Y. But concluding that there is no relationship is obviously incorrect. There appears to be a strong relationship, but the nature of the

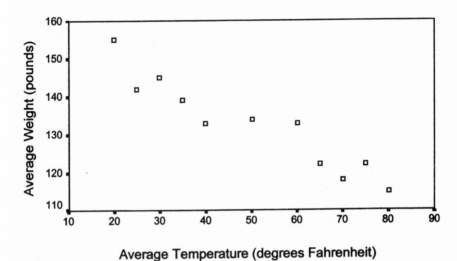

Average Temperature (degrees Fahrenheit)

Figure 8.3.   Scatter Plot of Average Temperature and Average Weight (Sample of 11 Hypothetical Populations).

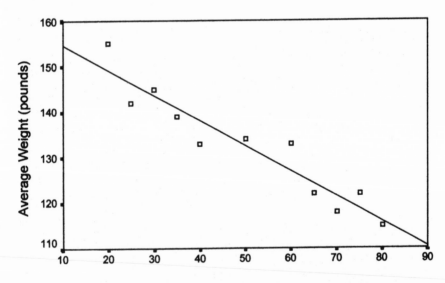

Average Temperature (degrees Fahrenheit)

Figure 8.4.   Line for Plot of Average Temperature and Average Weight.

relationship is not described by a straight line. Most statistical programs allow you to try to fit other curves to your data; the significance of these fits can also be determined. Figure 8.6 shows the fit of a quadratic equation, which appears to fit quite well. The associated p-value is .0005, which means that the chance of getting this result (if there were no quadratic relationship) is only 5 in 10,000.

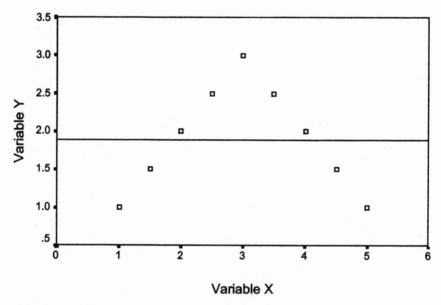

Figure 8.5.   Linear Fit to a Nonlinear Relationship.

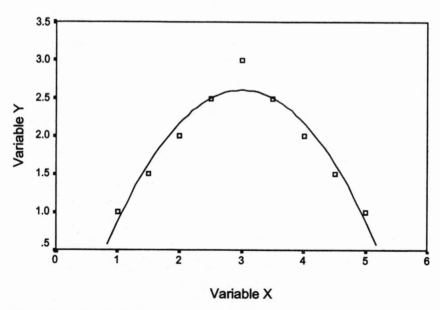

Figure 8.6.   Quadratic Fit to a Nonlinear Relationship.

Ordinal Variables

Suppose you want to know if there is a relationship between two variables, each of which is measured on an ordinal scale. There are several nonparametric measures of association, each of which can be tested for statistical significance. Like Pearson's r, each of these measures provides a coefficient that varies between 0.00 and ±1.00. Tests of significance give probability values for the likelihood that these coefficients (or larger ones) would occur by chance, if there were no associations between the variables. The most commonly used measures are:

- *Spearman's rho;*
- *Kendall's tau* (which is more appropriate when ties in rank are numerous); and
- *Gamma* (which can also be used, as we have noted, to measure the association in a contingency table with ordered rows and columns).

Recall that we discussed gamma when we talked about measures of association for 2 by 2 tables. Phi coefficients can reach 1.00 only when all the cases are on one diagonal. Gamma will reach 1.00 with one zero cell. If your theoretical model suggests that X is *either* a necessary *or* a sufficient cause of Y (but not necessary *and* sufficient), gamma may be the appropriate choice. So, as we see in tables 8.7a and 8.7b, table 8.7a would have a rho, tau, and gamma of 1.00. But for table 8.7b, only gamma would be 1.00. Gamma goes to 1 when the cells on one side of the diagonal are empty, just as in table 8.7b where the cells below the diagonal are empty. Because of this characteristic, gamma usually gives you a higher coefficient than rho or tau for the same table. Your decision as to which measure to use for an association between ordinal variables should depend on what kind of association you theoretically expect, not on the fact that gamma would give you a larger coefficient.

Multivariate Analyses

All of the analyses we have discussed so far consider the relationship between two variables. Usually one is considered a possible cause and the other the possible effect. But often a researcher has reason to believe that more than one variable is possibly a cause. One of the most common situations is when previous research has supported a particular factor as a possible cause and a new researcher thinks that an additional factor is involved. The first step might be to see if the new factor also predicts by itself. If it does, the second step is to compare how well the new factor predicts, when its effect is compared with that of the previously suspected

Table 8.7a.	All Cases on Diagonal.		
	Y *Rank 1*	*Y* *Rank 2*	*Y* *Rank 3*
X Rank 1	10		
X Rank 2		15	
X Rank 3			20

Table 8.7b.	No Cases below Diagonal.		
	Y *Rank 1*	*Y* *Rank 2*	*Y* *Rank 3*
X Rank 1	8	2	2
X Rank 2		10	5
X Rank 3			20

factor. In short, what we need this time around is an analysis that considers the possible independent effects of two or more variables on the dependent variable.

The type of analysis one can do depends once again on how the variables are measured. For instance, multiple regression is supposed to have an interval dependent variable, but the test may be robust enough to permit the dependent variable to be ordinal if it has a considerable number of ordered scale scores (see Labovitz 1967, 1970). In addition, some of the independent variables may be "dummy variables," that is, dichotomized nominal variables. Other independent variables may be ordinal. Another possibility is to use analysis of variance models that can have interval as well as nominal variables as the independent variables.

Multivariate analyses are complex. The reader should look at textbooks in multivariate analysis for further information. Such analyses allow us to measure the strength of a particular relationship, and to compare it with the strength of other relationships. How much does each independent variable predict, controlling on the effects of the other independent variables?

NOTES

1. The formulas for variance and standard deviation are divided by $n-1$ if you are calculating them to estimate the population from a sample; they are divided by n if you are dealing with the population.

2. A two-way analysis of variance allows for evaluating the effects of two nominal variables on a dependent variable that is an interval scale, but we will not discuss this type of analysis here.

3. The computations can be done without computers, but now these computations are rarely done without computer assistance.

4. Deviations are squared to eliminate negative numbers.

9

Reliability

Reliability refers to consistency or stability in measurement. There are many aspects of reliability. Many processes are involved in measurement and there are many different types of situations in which measurement takes place. If a test is supposed to measure some enduring characteristic of an individual, it should give approximately the same result when that individual is tested again. This is referred to as **test-retest reliability**. If two observers watch the same scene in order to record certain actions of individuals, reliability means that the different coders record the same actions similarly. This is **inter-observer reliability**. If two coders independently try to measure something in the same material, whether it be a passage from ethnography, an observation protocol, or an interview, reliability means that the coders assign approximately the same score. This is **inter-rater reliability**.

It is obvious that a researcher cannot achieve reliability in any sense without good measurement design. If a test is supposed to measure some enduring characteristic of an individual, but the results differ from day to day, then the test is probably not measuring what it is supposed to measure. If two observers or coders read the same material and fail to assign the same scale score, it could be because the rating instructions were not clear enough. However, not all unreliability is due to measurement design. Other factors can lower reliability, such as one observer does not pay enough attention to something or one of the observers is seriously biased. But almost always, an unreliable measure cannot be a valid measure.[1] If we think of the valid score as the "true" score, any departures from that score, even departures due to unreliability, would decrease the validity of the measure.

While an unreliable measure almost always cannot be a valid measure, a reliable measure is not necessarily a valid measure. If we were to take temperature readings hourly on January 1 to measure the average temperature in the winter, there could be reliable readings by two different observers, but the measure would not likely be a valid measure of average *winter* temperature. Temperature in almost all climates fluctuates considerably over three months.

ASSESSING RELIABILITY

Reliability is not an all or nothing thing. No one expects perfect replication all the time. What we seek are measures with a high *degree* of reliability. The higher the reliability, the better. There is no absolute standard for acceptable reliability, but researchers should always strive, if possible, to make a reliability assessment and report the degree of reliability obtained.[2] As we will see later, there is considerable benefit to be gained if all the cases and all the variables are rated independently by two observers. However, it is acceptable to assess reliability for only a proportion of the cases, if those cases are chosen randomly. Otherwise, the reliability check might be biased.

There are two common methods used to assess inter-rater reliability in cross-cultural research. Each has its advantages and disadvantages.

Percentage of Agreement

This method can be used only when the variable has a discrete number of scale positions or scores. For example, a scale might be a presence/absence scale, or it might be an ordinal scale with up to five scale positions. There is bound to be some unreliability when the variable has a very large number of possible scores. For each variable, a datasheet shows all the cases rated by both Rater 1 and Rater 2. Table 9.1 shows the scores that each rater gave for two different variables rated on three-point scales (Variables 1 and Variable 2) for a sample of ten cases. The disagreements are in boldface. There are two disagreements for Variable 1 (case 4 and case 8) and two disagreements for Variable 2 (case 3 and case 5). (For now, ignore the possibility that one or both raters said they could not rate the case; we will return to this issue later.) To obtain the percentage of agreement, you count the number of agreements and divide that number by the number of cases rated by both raters. With eight agreements and ten cases, the percentage of agreement is the same in both examples. Notice, however, that the two errors for Variable 1 are more serious than for Variable 2. This is because in the errors for Variable 1 the two raters code the same case on the opposite ends of the scale (suppose 1 = rare; 2 = occasional; and 3 = frequent); for Variable 2, the two raters disagree, but give contiguous scores (1 and 2; 2 and 3). The percentage of agreement method cannot convey the degree of discrepancy between the ratings, which is a disadvantage. As we shall see shortly, the next method would give us additional information about the degree to which the two sets of ratings are the same or close, which provides a more accurate way to assess reliability.

With a larger number of cases, the data for Rater 1 and Rater 2 would be entered into a computer and the researcher could subtract the absolute difference (disregarding the direction of difference) between the two scores for each variable. Anything other than a zero would be a disagreement. The number of zeros indicates the number of agreements. With a large number of cases and limited scoring possibilities, it is preferable to prepare a table to examine the relationship between the two raters' ratings. (This method is called cross-tabulation or cross-tabs in most statistical programs.) Tables 9.2a and 9.2b show the pattern of agreement for two raters on Variables 3 and 4 for 100 cases. Once again, in both tables there is the same percentage of agreement—82 percent, but table 9.2a shows a more serious pattern of errors because the raters disagree to the maximum extent in the nineteen disagreements.

Coefficient of Association

Most coefficients of association are designed to convey the degree to which one variable predicts another. As we saw in chapter 8, coefficients usually vary from −1.00 to +1.00. We would never expect a minus

Table 9.1.   Agreement between Rater 1 and Rater 2 on Variable 1 and Variable 2

	Rater 1 (Variable 1)	Rater 2 (Variable 1)		Rater 1 (Varaible 2)	Rater 2 (Variable 2)
Case 1	1	1	Case 1	1	1
Case 2	3	3	Case 2	3	3
Case 3	2	2	Case 3	1	2
Case 4	1	3	Case 4	2	2
Case 5	1	1	Case 5	3	2
Case 6	2	2	Case 6	1	1
Case 7	3	3	Case 7	3	3
Case 8	3	1	Case 8	2	2
Case 9	2	2	Case 9	1	1
Case 10	1	1	Case 10	3	3

Percentage of Agreement = 8/10 or 80% = 8/10 or 80%
Correlation Coefficient (Pearson's r) = .42 (n.s.) = .87 (p <.005, one tail)

Table 9.2a. Relationship between Two Raters' Ratings of Variable 3			

	Rater 2		
Rater 1	Score 1	Score 2	Score 3	Total
---	---	---	---	---
Score 1	26	0	9	35
Score 2	0	30	0	30
Score 3	9	0	26	35
Total	35	30	35	100

Percentage of agreement = 82%

Table 9.2b. Relationship between Two Raters' Ratings of Variable 4			

	Rater 2		
Rater 1	Score 1	Score 2	Score 3	Total
---	---	---	---	---
Score 1	26	9	0	35
Score 2	0	30	0	30
Score 3	0	9	26	35
Total	26	48	26	100

Percentage of agreement = 82%

sign for reliability because it conveys that if one rater gives a low score, the other rater is likely to give a high score. What we want is a high positive coefficient—the higher, the better. If we had computed a correlation coefficient for the relationship between the raters' ratings for Variables 1 and 2 in table 9.1, we would have detected that the relationship between Rater 1's and Rater 2's ratings was stronger for Variable 2, where the discrepant ratings were adjacent scores, than for Variable 1, where the discrepant scores were far apart. (The respective correlation coefficients are .42 and .87, even though the percentage of agreement is the same.) It is in this sense that the correlation coefficient gives us more information than the percentage of agreement. However, there is one mathematical property of most correlation coefficients that would mislead us with respect to reliability. It is possible to obtain a perfect correlation even when the two raters do not ever agree. This possibility is shown in tables 9.3a and 9.3b. If we computed a Pearson's r or a Spearman's rho, we would get a perfect positive correlation for *both* tables. This is because in both tables the ratings of one rater *perfectly* predict the other rater's ratings in a linear order. That is exactly what the two correlation coefficients measure. In table 9.3a, though, the two raters never agree. There is a systematic bias on the part of at least one of the raters. When Rater 1 says 1, Rater 2 says 2. When Rater 1 says 2, Rater 2 says 3. The two raters are interpreting the material to be coded in different ways. Both sets of scores cannot be correct—either one of the raters is inflating the frequency or the other rater is deflating the frequency. If we computed a percentage of agreement, we would get 0 percent for table 9.3a and 100 percent for table 9.3b. Whether or not a researcher need be concerned about the disagreements depends upon the goal of the research. If the goal is to summarize the frequency of a pattern around the world using a five-point scale (with 1 being rare and 5 being almost always), the inflation or deflation of frequency by one of the raters would be serious. However, if a researcher's goal is to test a hypothesis about the relationship between two variables (suppose the researcher were investigating the relationship between variables 3 and 4), the systematic error on one variable would not matter much.

Advantages and Disadvantages of Both Methods

As the examples above show, both methods of computing reliability have their advantages and disadvantages, which is a problem demanding a solution. The percentage agreement method conveys any discrepancy, however slight, between raters. Its disadvantage is that it doesn't provide a measure of the seriousness of the discrepancy. The correlation coefficient method gives lower scores if the two raters' scores are far from the line of best fit. However, the correlation coefficient does not distinguish between perfect agreement and systematic bias on the part of the raters.

An obvious solution to the problem is to compute reliability by *both* methods. Using both methods will give the researcher a lot more information. In any case, the researcher should always examine the pattern of discrepancies.

WHAT TO DO ABOUT DISCREPANCIES

It is one thing to analyze the degree of reliability; it is another to decide what to do about discrepancies. There are three commonly used methods: (1) using one rater's ratings; (2) summing or averaging the two sets; and (3) resolving the disagreements. We advocate another method: (4) omitting those cases that have been less reliably rated.

Table 9.3a. Relationship between Two Raters' Scores on Variable 5

Rater 1	1	2	3	4	5	
1	0	0	0	0	0	0
2	25	0	0	0	0	25
3	0	25	0	0	0	25
4	0	0	25	0	0	25
5	0	0	0	25	0	25
Total	25	25	25	25	0	100

Percentage of agreement = 0 percent
Pearson's r = 1.00

Table 9.3b. Relationship between Two Raters' Scores on Variable 6

Rater 1	1	2	3	4	5	
1	20	0	0	0	0	0
2	0	20	0	0	0	20
3	0	0	20	0	0	20
4	0	0	0	20	0	20
5	0	0	0	0	20	20
Total	25	25	25	25	0	100

Percentage of agreement = 100 percent
Pearson's r = 1.00

Using One Rater's Codings

If a reliability check is done with only a small proportion of the cases (the second rater has been asked to rate only some of the cases) and it is acceptably high, there is no choice but to use the ratings by the person who rated all of the cases. Sometimes, if both raters have rated all cases, a researcher will decide to use the ratings of the person who is arguably likely to be a better rater because of previous experience, additional education, or evidence of more careful work, such as taking more notes or paying more attention to instructions. If there are only two raters, however, it may be quite judgmental to say which person is better. If there are three or more raters, the raters can be compared with each other. If one person's ratings do not correlate well with the ratings by either of the other coders, the chances are good that the first person is not a good rater. Even if the researcher wants to use one set of ratings, it is probably a good idea to show that the results are still significant (albeit less so) when another rater's ratings are used.

Summing or Averaging

Summing or averaging a set of scores from two raters (or even three) results in a new score that gives equal weight to the different raters. Mathematically it doesn't matter whether the sum or average is used, but the average score is more interpretable because it uses the same metric or system of measurement as the originally designed score. There are two main advantages of this method. First, it is less judgmental and therefore objectively fairer, since it gives both raters an equal voice. Second, if each rater's score is thought of as a separate measure, the combined score (average or sum) should be closer to the "true" score. Rosenthal and Rosnow (1984) show that if a correlation coefficient between two raters' scores is .75, the reliability of the mean scores is actually .86.

There are two situations where averaging or summing would not be preferable. The first is if there is an objective reason for expecting that one rater produced more valid measures. If you sum or average the scores from a better rater with those from a less competent rater, you may increase the error. A second reason would be that discussing the disagreements could result in a more valid measure, according to some external criterion. In cases where a measure requires reading, interpreting, and synthesizing a lot of material, talking with the other rater might lead to one of the raters being shown information (previously missed by that rater) that would allow the raters to agree on a rating.

Resolution Method

Sometimes it pays to let raters discuss their disagreements. This is especially important in the pretesting phases of a project. If a researcher sits in on the discussions, he or she may learn that the raters are disagreeing because they are interpreting the coding rules differently. Such disagreements may lead to spelling out the rules in more informative ways. As mentioned above, resolution may be especially important when the material that needs to be read is complex and voluminous. Sometimes one rater will simply say, "Oh, if I had seen that passage, I would have rated the case the same as you did." Averaging or summing the scores would not allow the raters to change their minds and perhaps come up with a more valid score. The major disadvantage of the resolution method is that status differential or force of personality alone can affect the resolution process. Suppose one of the raters is the professor and the other rater is a student. While it is possible that the resolution process would be perfectly objective, some students would be intimidated and likely to agree with the professor. It is possible to see if one rater is influencing the resolution process more often than the other rater. If you look at the original score and the resolved score, you can see if one rater changed much more than the other.[3]

Does the fact that one rater influences the other necessarily mean that it is status or force of personality that influences the decision? Not necessarily. It is possible that one of the two is more careful and finds more relevant information. It is difficult to distinguish power from knowledge in assessing the degree to which one rater affects another in resolving disagreements.

Dropping Serious Disagreements

We advocate another method for resolving discrepancies. We think researchers should deal with the fact that two raters disagree considerably on a particular score. Rather than ignore that fact by averaging or attempting a resolution, it might be more legitimate to consider that fact in the analysis. After all, if one rater says a case does not have a trait, and another says it does, it is likely that the material being read was ambiguous at the very least. It would be difficult to say which score was the correct one, including the average score. To include a case with an extreme disagreement is only likely to create more error, with the possible exception of one rater changing a rating based on information the other rater saw. The disadvantage of dropping cases with serious disagreement is that we lose cases for analysis. In our experience, this disadvantage is more than compensated by the improvement in predictability that usually results when the cases with serious disagreements are omitted from the analysis.

But it is not necessary to drop cases. Perhaps the best way of handling disagreements is to create a reliability score for each case and each variable. If you leave out cases where one rater declined to make a rating, the score can simply be the absolute value of the discrepancy between the two raters, ranging from 0 (indicating no discrepancy) to whatever number is the maximum discrepancy possible (on a five-point scale it would be four points). With such a reliability scale, one can reanalyze the findings with different degrees of reliability. So, for example, one could use all of the cases for an analysis and then take out those with serious disagreements and analyze the data again. If taking out such cases fails to make much difference, they can all be left in.

This method can also be combined with other methods. That is, if there are ratings by two raters, one could use one person's ratings, average the two or resolve them, and still take out unreliable cases to see if it makes a difference.

NOTES

1. If two interviewers of different gender get different answers from the same person, the lack of reliability may reflect a valid difference in how a person responds to the gender of the interviewer.

2. Lack of funding for a project always makes it difficult to get inter-rater reliability. Researchers should consider asking for reciprocal help from another researcher.

3. Rohner and Rohner (1981) suggest that McNemar's test for the significance of changes can be used to test for the significance of the difference in the influence of Rater 1 versus Rater 2.

10

Summing Up

The basic assumption of cross-cultural research is that comparison is possible because patterns (kinds of phenomena) that occur repeatedly can be identified. These patterns or variables can be measured as present or absent, or in terms of the degree to which they are present. Even the most qualitative phenomena can be measured, often ordinally. Cross-culturalists believe that all generalizations require testing, no matter how plausible we may think they are. This requirement applies to descriptive generalizations as well as to presumed relationships or associations. If a theory or hypothesis has merit, the presumed causes and the presumed effect should be significantly (and strongly) associated synchronically. This is the usual kind of association tested cross-culturally. A synchronic association involves variables that are measured for the same time or period for a given sample case. If a synchronic test is successful, we might try to make a diachronic test (measuring the independent variables for earlier times). Usually a causal theory presumes that causes will precede their effect.

TYPES OF CROSS-CULTURAL COMPARISONS

Cross-cultural comparisons vary in three ways: (1) worldwide versus regional; (2) using secondary versus primary data; and (3) synchronic or diachronic. Each of these dimensions has its advantages and disadvantages. The results of any kind of worldwide cross-cultural research are the most likely to be generalizable to the universe of cultures around the world.

They also are based on the broadest range of cultural variability. A researcher who is familiar with a particular region knows a lot about the history and the details of particular cultures in that region. Such knowledge may be especially helpful if a theory or hypothesis is not supported in a worldwide comparison. Historical or diachronic comparisons can help researchers assess whether the presumed causes change before their presumed effects. But historical comparisons are usually more difficult or time-consuming to conduct, so we recommend that synchronic tests should be made first. Comparisons employing primary field data are the most expensive and time-consuming and should be undertaken only when the necessary data are not already available. See the decision tree in Box 1.1 (in chapter 1) to help decide what type of comparison is most feasible or preferable.

STEPS IN A CROSS-CULTURAL STUDY

1. Ask a clear *one-sentence* research question. The type of question largely determines the nature of the research. The four major types of questions are: (1) descriptive; (2) causal; (3) consequence; and (4) nondirectional relational. Pick a question you really want to answer!
2. Formulate at least one hypothesis to test. A hypothesis specifies the expected statistical association(s) between two or more variables. Hypotheses are derived logically from theories.
3. Operationalize each variable in the hypothesis. Not only does this mean that the researcher should define the variable. The researcher also needs to give precise instructions on how to decide where a case falls on that variable. Usually this requires making up a scale and giving instructions for how to code each point on that scale. All scales should be pretested by the researcher. Coding rules may need more specification or simplification.
4. To minimize error, strive for measures that are more direct conceptually, require relatively little inference on the part of coders, and specify a time and a place focus. If possible, you should use more than one coder, who should not know the hypotheses to be tested. With more than one coder you can test for reliability and possibly eliminate the cases with less reliable ratings. Data quality codes can be constructed for each variable and the results can be reanalyzed omitting the poorer quality data.
5. Since there is no complete list as yet of the world's described cultures, which you could randomly sample from, you need to choose a sampling frame that is reasonably representative. Table 6.1 (in

chapter 6) lists the commonly used samples in secondary cross-cultural comparisons. If you want to use some of the data already coded for one of the available samples, by all means use that sample as your sampling frame. But use some kind of probabilistic sampling strategy to choose cases from that sampling frame. If you want to code variables yourself, the HRAF Collection of Ethnography facilitates that task. The electronic version (eHRAF Ethnography), even though it does not contain as many cases as the entire Collection, is the most efficient way to search the ethnographic record to make coding decisions. But your institution has to be a member of the HRAF consortium if you want to access eHRAF Ethnography.

6. Test the statistical significance of your results, and if possible evaluate the strength of the obtained associations. Of course, you will be pleased if the results are statistically significant. But do not be too pleased! Remember that support for a hypothesis does not prove the theory from which it is derived. If the results are consistent with the theory, all that we can say is that the theory is supported by the results. Ideally, to increase our confidence about the validity of a theory, we should try to replicate it with different samples and different types of study (e.g., historical, intrasocietal comparisons, experimental).

7. If your hypothesis is not supported, you should question the plausibility of the theory from which the hypothesis was derived. However, it is also important to reexamine your research design. Were the measures measuring what they were supposed to? Did you use multiple measures? Might there be factors that you didn't consider that could have masked your expected results? In our experience, it is important to think about why results did not turn out as expected. You might still be right, but only partially.

In sum, we hope that we have persuaded you that cross-cultural research is not only necessary for validating theory universally, but it is also not that hard to do. And it is often exhilarating. So go to it and enjoy!

Appendix

Using the Human Relations Area Files

There are now two HRAF collections. The original one, the HRAF Collection of Ethnography, has been expanded and updated annually since 1949; it covers 365 cultures as of 2000. The HRAF Collection of Archaeology, which also grows annually, first became available in 1999; it covers twenty major archaeological traditions—and many more subtraditions and sites—as of 2000. Researchers affiliated with institutions belonging to the HRAF consortium for a particular collection can now access some or all of that collection on the World Wide Web. The archaeology collection (eHRAF Archaeology) is posted in its entirety on the Web. The ethnography collection is not yet completely posted on the Web. As of 2000, eHRAF Ethnography covers seventy-eight cultures around the world, including twelve North American immigrant cultures. From ten to fifteen cultures—and some 40,000 pages—are added each year to eHRAF Ethnography. Some of the cultures added are new to the collection, and some are converted and updated from the microfiche version of the collection. About 10,000 new pages, covering about ten major archaeological traditions (and even more subtraditions and sites), are added each year to eHRAF Archaeology. When you try to use any version of the HRAF Collections for the first time, remember that not all cultures and traditions are included.

Books, articles, and other materials that describe cultures are widely scattered and often inaccessible, and expensive to assemble and utilize effectively. This is why HRAF was invented in the first place. But HRAF doesn't just assemble materials. It also makes search and retrieval easy by subject-indexing to the paragraph level all the assembled information. We focus here on the Collection of Ethnography, because most cross-cultural research uses data from ethnography. But it should be noted that the Collection of Archaeology is modeled in nearly all respects on the Collection of Ethnography.

Development of the HRAF Collections began with the belief that valid generalizations about human behavior and culture are most likely to emerge from comparative research on the varying lifestyles of peoples around the world. In 1937, at the Yale Institute of Human Relations, a small group of researchers under the direction of the Institute's Director, Mark A. May, and anthropologist George Peter Murdock attempted to design a system for classifying (indexing) the cultural, behavioral, and background information on the world's societies. This unique indexing system is known as the *Outline of Cultural Materials* or OCM.

The HRAF Collection of Ethnography mostly contains primary source materials—published books and articles, but also including some unpublished manuscripts and dissertations—on selected cultures or societies representing all major regions of the world. The materials are organized and indexed according to the OCM for rapid and accurate retrieval of specific data on particular cultures and topics. The HRAF collections of subject-indexed data deliver information in a manner that *significantly increases the accessibility of the original source materials.* Over the years the media has changed—from paper files to microfiche to CD-ROM and now the World Wide Web. Until 1958, the HRAF Collection was produced and distributed as paper files: source materials were reproduced on 5" x 8" paper slips that were indexed by subject (OCM) category and filed by culture. Wider distribution of the collection was facilitated in 1958 with the development of the HRAF Microfiles Program. Materials from the paper files were processed into microfiche and issued in annual installments to an increasing number of member institutions. Installment 42 in 1994 was the last microfiche series issued to members. As of 2000, eHRAF Ethnography provides updated data on the sixty-culture Probability Sample Files (PSF), in addition to other cultures. The first six installments of eHRAF Ethnography (1995–2000) total nearly one quarter of a million pages of fully indexed ethnographic materials.

If a particular culture or tradition is in the files, all of the documents pertaining to it are geographically labeled according to a unique code called the *Outline of World Cultures* (OWC). Cultures are classified according to geographical regions:

A = Asia;
E = Europe;
F = Africa (sub-Saharan);
M = Middle East and North Africa;

N = North America;
O = Oceania;
R = Eurasia (cultures located in the former Soviet Union);
S = South America.

Note that in the past Muslim societies in sub-Saharan Africa were given OWC numbers starting with M.

All the cultures in the Collection of Ethnography are classified in terms of these eight regions. Thus, all the documents pertaining to sub-Saharan African cultures are grouped by culture and their OWC alphanumeric identification begins with "F." Each of the major regions is then subdivided into subregions or countries designated by a second letter: for example, "RB" for the Baltic countries; "FF" for the country of Nigeria and its component cultural units. So, in the subregion labeled "NM" (Middle Atlantic States) of North America, "NM09" refers to the Iroquois. Similarly, "FL12" refers to the Maasai culture in the country Kenya (L) in Africa. Thus, a culture covered in the collection may be labeled regionally, subregionally, and politically, as well as by its name.

Of the more than two thousand cultures listed in the OWC, 365 are now covered in the Collection of Ethnography, including the seventy-eight in eHRAF Ethnography. The 365 probably constitute about 40 percent of the well-described cultures in the world. The cultures in the collection have been mainly selected in the past on the basis of the following criteria:

1. *Maximizing cultural diversity.* The cultures should represent, as far as possible, the known range and variety of cultural types in terms of language, history, economy, and social organization.
2. *Maximizing geographical dispersal.* The cultures should be representative of all major world regions and all major ecological settings.
3. *Adequacy of literature.* Consistent with the two preceding criteria, the literature on a culture should describe many aspects of life.

Below is the numerical distribution of the cultures in the entire HRAF Collection of Ethnography, according to geographic region (not OWC letters):

Africa 41
Asia 70
Europe 27
Middle East 31
North America 84
Oceania 42
Eurasia 19
South America 51

By 2001, new cases will be added by simple random sampling from an expanded OWC, now being constructed at HRAF.

Once the decision has been reached to build a file on a particular culture, extensive bibliographic research by HRAF staff, usually with advice from a regional specialist, identifies the most important literature to be included on that culture.

The full-text materials processed for the Collection of Ethnography are largely descriptive rather than theoretical, with the great majority being primary documents that are based on field observation. The ideal ethnography consists of a detailed description of the culture, or of a particular community or region within that culture, written on the basis of prolonged residence among the people by a professional anthropologist or other social scientist. Other kinds of documents are included in the Collection of Ethnography because they provide important sets of information not otherwise available; these documents may be the only sources available for particular time periods, regions, or subject matter. Thus the collection for each culture may contain documents written by travelers, missionaries, colonial officials, and traders, as well as by anthropologists.

For some cultures, the literature is so extensive that only the most significant works can be processed. This is the case with the Saami or Lapps (OWC code EP04). On the other hand, the literature written on some cultures is rather limited, as for the Andamans (OWC code AZ02), in which case it is likely that nearly all of the available material has been processed.

A page in a document may include many OCM subject categories. The page would then be indexed according to the appropriate OCM category codes (see Murdock et al. 2000); the subject codes are referred to as OCM numbers. The OCM consists of more than 700 subject categories plus a category numbered "000" for unclassified materials. The subject categories are grouped into nearly ninety major divisions, each assigned a three-digit code ranging from 100 (Orientation) to 910 (Archaeological Measures, Techniques, and Analyses). Within each major subject division, more specific categories are defined. For example, the 590 (Family) division is subdivided into seven more specific subject categories as follows: 591 (Residence), 592 (Household), 593 (Family Relationships), 594 (Nuclear Family), 595 (Polygamy), 596 (Extended Families), and 597 (Adoption). Following the number and title of each category in the OCM is a brief descriptive statement indicating the range of information that may be classified under that category. Beneath this statement is usually a list of cross-references to other categories under which related information may be classified.

The reader should note that the OCM contains an extensive index to the subject categories that can direct researchers to the particular OCM numbers that are relevant to their interests. So, for example, if you want to measure the degree to which women are cloistered, you would see in the index to the OCM that categories 562 (Sex Status) and 837 (Extramarital Sex Relations) would give you relevant information.

The only kind of search possible in the microfiche version of the collection is by OCM category. After choosing your cultures and OCM categories, browse through the selected file pages to find appropriate material. Classification of the text may sometimes be done sentence by sentence, but most OCM numbers are assigned to paragraphs. Remember that HRAF contains many time and place foci, so only some of the documents may be appropriate to your research.

If you are using eHRAF you have more choices in searching. You can search by an exact word, if the topic you are looking for is aptly as well as frequently described by that word (e.g., tattoo, or irrigat [truncated for irrigation or irrigate]). However, most topics you will be interested in cannot be easily found by word searches. Therefore, the OCM search is generally the search method of choice. *If you were to search by words only, you might not find what you are looking for because the authors did not use those words or the source is in another language. Or there might be too many irrelevant hits because the words are used in many more contexts than the one you are interested in.* You can also combine word searches and OCM searches in Boolean, proximity, or basic word searches. For more information about the HRAF collections, see HRAF's home page at www.yale.edu/hraf.

Glossary

association—a relationship between variables that is supported by empirical research.

central tendency—a descriptive statistic that summarizes the center of the distribution with one number. The most common are the mean, the mode, and the median.

chi-square test—a significance test usually applied to contingency tables.

content validity—the degree to which a domain is sampled in designing a measure.

convergent validity—independent measures of the same concept are shown to be related.

contingency table—a table consisting of rows displaying variability in one variable and columns displaying variability in a second variable that shows the frequency of cases in each combination of values.

dependent variable—the trait to be explained.

descriptive statistics—statistics that are used to summarize data to make them comprehensible.

diachronic comparison—comparison over different time periods.

disproportionate stratified sampling—some subgroups are overrepresented and others are underrepresented. If the sampling is based on probability methods, there is a known probability that a case will be chosen, although each case will not have an equal chance to be chosen.

eHRAF Archaeology—HRAF's electronic collection of archaeology.

eHRAF Ethnography—HRAF's electronic collection of ethnography.

face validity—little justification is needed to decide about the validity of a measure because "on the face of it" the measure measures what it is supposed to measure.

falsify—disconfirm.

Galton's Problem—the concern that historical relatedness between sample cases may account for a cross-cultural relationship between variables.

Guttman scale—a scale that conveys a hierarchy of traits so a case with a certain score has all the features of a case with a lower score.

HRAF Collection of Ethnography—the entire HRAF archive of ethnographic materials.

hypothesis (*plural*, hypotheses)—posits relationships between variables. Hypotheses are usually derived from theories. These hypotheses are what we test to falsify theories.

independent variable—a presumed cause.

inferential statistics—statistics that allow researchers to generalize their sample results to a larger universe, assuming that the sampling is unbiased and the research design is appropriate.

inter-observer reliability—the degree to which different observers see things similarly.

inter-rater reliability—the degree to which different coders code similarly.

interval measure—a measure that has equally spaced points but no true zero point.

law—a repeatedly replicated association that is accepted as true by most scientists.

marginal—a row or column total in a contingency table.

mean—the average score in a sample or population.

median—that score in a sample or population below and above which 50 percent of the scores fall.

mode—that score in a sample or population with the highest frequency.

nominal measure—a measure that divides cases into discrete, unambiguous sets or categories. In other words, the sets are said to be different.

nonparametric tests—sometimes called "distribution-free" tests, they do not require parametric assumptions about the data.

OCM (Outline of Cultural Materials)—the indexing system used in the HRAF collections to facilitate search and retrieval of information.

operational hypothesis—a hypothesis that is restated with an operational measure (procedure for measuring) for each of the variables.

ordinal measure—a measure that conveys order, or relative degrees, of a trait or variable.

OWC (Outline of World Cultures)—a large list of the world's cultures by region.

parametric tests—make certain assumptions about the underlying distributions, such as that the distribution is normally distributed.

population—the universe of cases to which one wants to generalize the sample results.

probability sampling—a type of sampling in which each case has a known (and nonzero) chance of being chosen.

proportionate stratified sampling—each subgroup is represented in proportion to its occurrence in the total population. With random sampling from each stratum, each case in a stratum has an equal chance to be chosen.

random error—error in any and all directions.

range—the difference between the highest and the lowest scores in a sample or population.

ratio measure—a measure that has equally spaced intervals and a true zero point (i.e., the zero means that the trait is absent).

reliability—the degree of consistency or stability in a measure.

sampling frame—the list of units in the population that one actually samples from.

simple random sampling—a probability sample in which all cases have an equal chance to be chosen. Cases are drawn by a lottery method, using a table of random numbers, or by a random number generator in a statistical program.

standard deviation—the square root of the variance.

statistically significant—a result that is unlikely to be due to chance (conventionally with a p-value or probability of .05 or less).

stratified sampling—a sample is first divided into subgroups or strata and then cases are chosen from each stratum. In probability samples there is a known (and nonzero) probability of selection from each stratum. The two main types of stratified sampling are proportionate and disproportionate.

synchronic association—an association between variables measured for the same time per case.

synchronic comparison—a comparison of cases each of which is examined for the same time.

systematic error—unidirectional error that departs from the "true" score in a consistent way by either under- or overestimating the "true" score.

systematic sampling—a probability sample in which every nth case is chosen after a random start. All cases have an equal chance to be chosen.

test-retest reliability—the degree to which a second test replicates an earlier test.

theoretical hypothesis—a hypothesis that is stated in its more abstract (i.e., theoretical) form, without specifying measures.

theory—an explanation of a law or an association that contains some concepts that are, at least at the moment, not directly verifiable.

units of analysis—the studied units (e.g., families, individuals, communities, societies, countries).

validity—the degree to which a measure measures what it purports to measure.

variable—a trait that varies in degree or state.

variance—a measure of variability that is the average of the squared deviations between each score and the mean.

References

Barry, Herbert, III, Lili Josephson, Edith Lauer, and Catherine Marshall. 1977. Agents and techniques for child training; cross-cultural codes 6. *Ethnology* 16:191–230.

Barry, Herbert, III, and Alice Schlegel, eds. 1980. *Cross-cultural samples and codes*. Pittsburgh: University of Pittsburgh.

Bernard, H. Russell. 1994. *Research Methods in Anthropology: Qualitative and Quantitative Approaches*, 2d ed. Walnut Creek, Calif.: AltaMira Press.

Blalock, Hubert M., Jr. 1968. The measurement problem: a gap between the languages of theory and research. In *Methodology in social research*, ed. Hubert M. Blalock Jr. and Ann B. Blalock, 5–27. New York: McGraw-Hill.

———. 1972. *Social statistics*. 2d ed. New York: McGraw-Hill.

Bohannan, Paul, and Laura Bohannan. 1958. Tiv ethnography. Unpublished manuscript. New Haven, Conn: Human Relations Area Files (HRAF Source 22 in the Tiv file).

Bradley, Candice. 1987. Women, children and work. Ph.D. dissertation. Irvine: University of California.

———. 1989. Reliability and inference in the cross-cultural coding process. *Journal of Quantitative Anthropology* 1:353–71.

Broude, Gwen J., and Sarah J. Greene. 1983. Cross-cultural codes on husband-wife relationships. *Ethnology* 22:263–80.

Burton, Michael L. 1996. Constructing a scale of female contributions to agriculture: Methods for imputing missing data. *Cross-Cultural Research* 30:3–23.

Burton, Michael L., Carmella C. Moore, John W. M. Whiting, and A. Kimball Romney. 1996. Regions based on social structure. *Current Anthropology* 37:87–123.

Burton, Michael, and Douglas R. White. 1987. Cross-cultural surveys today. *Annual Reviews of Anthropology* 16:143–60.

———. 1991. Regional comparisons, replications, and historical network analysis. (Special issue. Cross-cultural and comparative research: theory and method.) *Behavior Science Research* 25:55–78.

Campbell, Donald T. 1961. The mutual methodological relevance of anthropology and psychology. In *Psychological anthropology: Approaches to culture and personality*, ed. Francis L. K. Hsu, 333–52. Homewood, Ill.: Dorsey Press.

Campbell, Donald T. 1988. *Methodology and epistemology for the social sciences: selected papers*, ed. E. Samuel Overton. Chicago: University of Chicago Press.

Campbell, Donald T., and Donald W. Fiske. 1959. Convergent and discriminant validation by the multitrait-multimethod matrix. *Psychological Bulletin* 56:81–105.

Carneiro, Robert L. 1970. Scale analysis, evolutionary sequences, and the rating of cultures. In *A handbook of method in cultural anthropology*, ed. Raoul Naroll and Ronald Cohen, 834–71. Garden City, N.Y.: Natural History Press.

Carneiro, Robert L., and Stephen F. Tobias. 1963. The application of scale analysis to the study of cultural evolution. *Transactions of the New York Academy of Sciences.* Ser. II, 26:196–207.

Cochran, William G. 1977. *Sampling techniques.* 3rd ed. New York: Wiley.

Cook, Thomas D., and Donald T. Campbell. 1979. *Quasi-experimentation: Design and analysis issues for field settings.* Chicago: Rand McNally.

D'Andrade, Roy. 1974. Memory and the assessment of behavior. In *Measurement in the social sciences*, ed. H. M. Blalock Jr., 149–86. Chicago: Aldine-Atherton.

Dickson, H. R. P. 1951. *The Arab of the desert: A glimpse into Badawin life in Kuwait and Sau'di Arabia.* London: George Allen & Unwin.

Divale, William T. 1974. Migration, external warfare, and matrilocal residence. *Behavior Science Research* 9:75–133.

———. 1975. Temporal focus and random error in cross-cultural hypothesis tests. *Behavior Science Research* 10:19–36.

———. 1976. Female status and cultural evolution: A study in ethnographer bias. *Behavior Science Research* 10:19–36.

Dorsey, George A., and James R. Murie, prepared for publication by Alexander Spoehr. 1940. Notes on Skidi Pawnee society. Chicago: Anthropological Series, Field Museum of Natural History, vol. 27, no. 2, pp. 65–119 (HRAF Source 5 in the Pawnee file).

Dow, Malcolm M. 1991. Statistical inference in comparative research: New directions. (Special issue. Cross-cultural and comparative research: Theory and method.) *Behavior Science Research* 25:235–57.

Dow, Malcolm M., Michael Burton, Douglas White, and Karl Reitz. 1984. Galton's problem as network autocorrelation. *American Ethnologist* 11:754–70.

Driver, Harold, and William C. Massey. 1957. Comparative studies of North American Indians. In *Transactions of the American Philosophical Society* 47: 165–456.

Eggan, Fred. 1954. Social anthropology and the method of controlled comparison. *American Anthropologist* 56:655–63.

Ember, Carol R. 1975. Residential variation among hunter-gatherers. *Behavior Science Research* 10:199–227.

———. 1978a. Men's fear of sex with women: A cross-cultural study. *Sex Roles: A Journal of Research* 4:657–78.

———. 1978b. Myths about hunter-gatherers. *Ethnology* 17:439–48.

———. 1981. A cross-cultural perspective on sex differences. In *Handbook of Cross-Cultural Human Development*, ed. Ruth H. Munroe, Robert L. Munroe, and Beatrice B. Whiting, 531–80. New York: Garland.

———. 1986. The quality and quantity of data for cross-cultural studies. *Behavior Science Research* 20:1–16.

———. 1990. Bibliography of cross-cultural methods. *Behavior Science Research* 24:141–54.

Ember, Carol R., with the assistance of Hugh Page Jr., Timothy O'Leary, and M. Marlene Martin. 1992. *Computerized concordance of cross-cultural samples*. New Haven, Conn.: Human Relations Area Files.

Ember, Carol R., and Melvin Ember. 1988. *Guide to cross-cultural research using the HRAF Archive*. New Haven, Conn.: Human Relations Area Files. See revised Web version at http://www.hraf.yale/hraf (under "Publications" or "Using the collections: Guide to cross-cultural research").

———. 1992a. Resource unpredictability, mistrust, and war: A cross-cultural study. *Journal of Conflict Resolution* 36:242–62.

———. 1992b. Warfare, aggression, and resource problems: Cross-cultural codes. *Behavior Science Research* 26:169–226.

———. 1996a. *Guide to cross-cultural research using the HRAF Archive*. New Haven, Conn.: Human Relations Area Files. A Web version may be downloaded from http://www.hraf.yale/hraf (under "Publications" or "Using the Collections: Guide to cross-cultural research").

———. 1996b. On cross-cultural research. In *Cross-cultural research for social science*, ed. Carol R. Ember and Melvin Ember. Upper Saddle River, N.J.: Prentice Hall, 107–26.

———. 1997. Violence in the ethnographic record: Results of cross-cultural research on war and aggression. In *Troubled times: Violence and warfare in the past*, ed. Debra L. Martin and David W. Frayer, 1–20. Langhorne, Pa.: Gordon and Breach Publishers.

———. 1998. Cross-Cultural Research. In *Handbook of Methods in Cultural Anthropology*. ed. H. Russell Bernard. Walnut Creek, Calif.: AltaMira Press.

———. 1999. *Anthropology*, 9th ed. Upper Saddle River, N.J.: Prentice Hall.

———. n.d. Father-absence and male aggression: A re-examination of the comparative evidence. Presented at the Invited Session for the Society for Psychological Anthropology "Childhood, Culture, Gender and Change: Papers in Honor of Beatrice Whiting." Organizers: Thomas S. Weisner and Susan Abbott-Jamieson. November 18, 1999. Chicago. In preparation as an article.

Ember, Carol R., Melvin Ember, and Bruce Russett. 1992. Peace between participatory polities: A cross-cultural test of the "democracies rarely fight each other" hypothesis. *World Politics* 44:573–99.

Ember, Carol R., and David Levinson. 1991. The substantive contributions of worldwide cross-cultural studies using secondary data. (Special issue. Cross-cultural and comparative research: Theory and method.) *Behavior Science Research* 25: 79–140.

Ember, Carol R., Marc H. Ross, Michael Burton, and Candice Bradley. 1991. Problems of measurement in cross-cultural research using secondary data. (Special issue. Cross-cultural and comparative research: Theory and method.) *Behavior Science Research* 25:187–216.

Ember, Carol R., Bruce Russett, and Melvin Ember. 1993. Political participation and peace: Cross-cultural codes. *Cross-Cultural Research* 27:97–145.

Ember, Melvin. 1970. Taxonomy in comparative studies. In *A handbook of method in cultural anthropology*, ed. Raoul Naroll and Ronald Cohen, 697–706. Garden City, N.Y.: Natural History Press.

———. 1971. An empirical test of Galton's problem. *Ethnology* 10:98–106.

———. 1974. Warfare, sex ratio, and polygyny. *Ethnology* 13:197–206.

———. 1984/85. Alternative predictors of polygyny. *Behavior Science Research* 19:1–23.

———. 1985. Evidence and science in ethnography: Reflections on the Freeman-Mead controversy. *American Anthropologist* 87:906–10.

———. 1991. The logic of comparative research. (Special issue. Cross-cultural and comparative research: Theory and method.) *Behavior Science Research* 25:143–53.

———. 1997. Evolution of the Human Relations Area Files. *Cross-Cultural Research* 31:3–15.

Ember, Melvin, and Carol R. Ember. 1971. The conditions favoring matrilocal residence versus patrilocal residence. *American Anthropologist* 73:571–94.

———. 1983. Male-female bonding: A cross-species study of mammals and birds. In *Marriage, family and kinship: Comparative studies of social organization*, by Melvin Ember and Carol R. Ember, 35–64. New Haven, Conn.: HRAF Press. Originally published in *Behavior Science Research* 14 (1979): 37–56.

———. 1995. Worldwide cross-cultural studies and their relevance for archaeology. *Journal of Archaeological Research* 3:87–111.

———. n.d. Why anthropological theory needs to be tested, why it needs to be tested cross-culturally, and why the "unit of analysis" problem is no problem. Unpublished paper.

Ember, Melvin, Carol R. Ember, and Bruce Russett. 1997. Inequality and democracy in the anthropological record. In *Inequality, democracy, and economic development*, ed. Manus Midlarsky, 110–30. Cambridge, Eng.: Cambridge University Press.

Ember, Melvin, and Keith F. Otterbein. 1991. Sampling in cross-cultural research. (Special issue. Cross-cultural and comparative research: theory and method.) *Behavior Science Research* 25:217–35.

Ethnographic atlas. 1962–. *Ethnology* 1:113ff. and intermittently thereafter.

Freeman, Linton. 1957. An empirical test of folk-urbanism. Ann Arbor: University of Michigan Microfilms, No. 23.

Galton, Francis. 1889. Comment in "Discussion" after Edward B. Tylor (1889).

Goldschmidt, Walter. 1965. Theory and strategy in the study of cultural adaptability. *American Anthropologist* 67:402–08.

Handwerker, W. Penn, and Stephen P. Borgatti. 1998. Reasoning with numbers. In *Handbook of methods in cultural anthropology*, ed. H. Russell Bernard, 549–93. Walnut Creek, Calif.: AltaMira Press.

Hempel, Carl G. 1965. *Aspects of scientific explanation*. New York: Free Press.

Hilger, M. Inez. 1951. Chippewa child life and its cultural background. Washington, D.C.: Government Printing Office (HRAF Source 15 in the Ojibwa file).

HRAF. 1967. The HRAF quality control sample universe. *Behavior Science Notes* 2:63–69.

Johnson, Allen. 1991. Regional comparative field research. (Special issue. Cross-cultural and comparative research: Theory and method.) *Behavior Science Research* 25:3–22.

Johnson, Allen, and Ross Sackett. 1998. Direct systematic observation of behavior. In *Handbook of methods in cultural anthropology*. ed. H. Russell Bernard, 301–31. Walnut Creek, Calif.: AltaMira Press.

Jorgensen, Joseph G. 1974. On continuous area and worldwide sample cross-cultural studies. In *Comparative studies by Harold E. Driver and essays in his honor*, ed. Joseph G. Jorgensen. New Haven, Conn.: HRAF Press.

Kalton, Graham. 1983. *Introduction to survey sampling*. Beverly Hills, Calif.: Sage.

Kish, Leslie. 1965. *Survey sampling*. New York: John Wiley.

———. 1987. *Statistical design for research*. New York: Wiley.

Kraemer, Helena Chmura, and Sue Theimann. 1987. *How many subjects? Statistical power analysis in research*. Newbury Park, Calif.: Sage.

Labovitz, Sanford. 1967. Some observations on measurement and statistics. *Social Forces* 46:151–60.

———. 1970. The assignment of numbers to rank order categories. *American Sociological Review* 35:515–24.

Lagacé, Robert O. 1979. The HRAF probability sample: Retrospect and prospect. *Behavior Science Research* 14:211–29.

Levinson, David. 1978. Holocultural studies based on the Human Relations Area Files. *Behavior Science Research* 13:295–302.

———. 1989. *Family violence in cross-cultural perspective*. Newbury Park, Calif.: Sage.

Marsh, Robert M. 1967. Appendices in *Comparative sociology: a codification of cross-societal analysis*. New York: Harcourt Brace & World.

Meggitt, M. J. 1964. Male-female relationships in the highlands of Australian New Guinea. *American Anthropologist* 66 (4, part 2):202–24.

Minturn, Leigh, and William W. Lambert. 1964. *Mothers of six cultures*. New York: Wiley.

Munroe, Robert L., Robert Hulefeld, James M. Rodgers, Damon L. Tomeo, and Steven K. Yamazaki. 2000. Aggression among children in four cultures. *Cross-Cultural Research* 43:3–25.

Munroe, Robert L., and Ruth H. Munroe. 1991a. Comparative field studies: Methodological issues and future possibilities. (Special issue. Cross-cultural and comparative research: Theory and method.) *Behavior Science Research* 25:155–85.

Munroe, Robert L., and Ruth H. Munroe. 1991b. Results of comparative field studies. (Special issue. Cross-cultural and comparative research: Theory and method.) *Behavior Science Research* 25:23–54.

Munroe, Robert L, and Ruth H. Munroe. 1992. Fathers in children's environments: A four culture study. In *Father-child relations*, ed. Barry S. Hewlett, 213–29. New York: Aldine de Gruyter.

Munroe, Ruth H., Robert L. Munroe, and Harold S. Shimmin. 1984. Children's work in four cultures: Determinants and consequences. *American Anthropologist* 86: 369–79.

Murdock, George P. 1949. *Social structure*. New York: Macmillan.

———. 1957. World ethnographic sample. *American Anthropologist* 59:664–87.

———. 1967. Ethnographic atlas: a summary. *Ethnology* 6:109–236.

———. 1981. *Atlas of world cultures*. Pittsburgh: University of Pittsburgh Press.

———. 1983. *Outline of World Cultures*, 6th rev. ed. New Haven, Conn.: Human Relations Area Files.

Murdock, George P., Clellan S. Ford, Alfred E. Hudson, Raymond Kennedy, Leo. W. Simmons, and John W. M. Whiting. 2000. *Outline of Cultural Materials*, 5th ed., revised 2000. New Haven, Conn.: Human Relations Area Files.

Murdock, George P., and Catarina Provost. 1973. Factors in the division of labor by sex: A cross-cultural analysis. *Ethnology* 12:203–25.

Murdock, George P., and Douglas R. White. 1969. Standard cross-cultural sample. *Ethnology* 8:329–69.

Musil, Alois. 1928. The manners and customs of the Rwala Bedouins. New York: American Geographical Society (HRAF Source 2 in the Rwala file).

Nadel, S. F. 1954. *Nupe religion*. London: Routledge & Kegan Paul.

Nagel, Ernest. 1961. The structure of science: Problems in the logic of scientific explanation. New York: Harcourt Brace & World.

Naroll, Raoul. 1956. A preliminary index of social development. *American Anthropologist* 58:687–715.

———. 1962. *Data quality control. A new research technique: prolegomena to a cross-cultural study of culture stress*. New York: Free Press.

———. 1967. The proposed HRAF probability sample. *Behavior Science Notes* 2:70–80.

———. 1970a. Galton's problem. In *A handbook of method in cultural anthropology*, eds. Raoul Naroll and Ronald Cohen, 974–89. Garden City, New York: Natural History Press.

———. 1970b. Data quality control in cross-cultural surveys. In *A handbook of method in cultural anthropology*, ed. Raoul Naroll and Ronald Cohen, 927–45. Garden City, N.Y.: Natural History Press.

———. 1977. Cost-effective research versus safer research. *Behavior Science Research* 11:123–48.

Naroll, Raoul, Vern L. Bullough, and Frada Naroll. 1974. Military deterrence in history: A pilot cross-historical survey. Albany: State University of New York Press.

Naroll, Raoul, and Richard G. Sipes. 1973. Standard ethnographic sample, 2d ed. *Current Anthropology* 14:111–40.

Naroll, Raoul, and Harold Zucker. 1974. Reply. *Current Anthropology* 15:316–17.

Nunnally, Jum C. 1978. *Psychometric theory*, 2d ed. New York: McGraw-Hill.

Pasternak, Burton, Carol R. Ember, and Melvin Ember. 1976. On the conditions favoring extended family households. *Journal of Anthropological Research* 32 (1976): 109-23. Reprinted in *Marriage, family and kinship: comparative studies of social organization*, by Melvin Ember and Carol R. Ember, 35–64. New Haven, Conn.: HRAF Press, 1983.

Pasternak, Burton, Carol R. Ember, and Melvin Ember. 1997. *Sex, gender, and kinship: A cross-cultural perspective*. Upper Saddle River, N.J.: Prentice Hall.

Pelto, Pertti J. 1962. Individualism in Skolt Lapp society. Helsinki: Suomen Muinaismuistoyhdistys (Finnish Antiquities Society) (HRAF Source 20 in Saami file).

Peregrine, Peter N., Carol R. Ember, and Melvin Ember. 2000. Comparative analyses of cultural evolution using eHRAF. Paper presented at annual meeting of the Society for American Archaeology, Philadelphia.

Popper, Karl. 1959. *Logic of scientific discovery*. New York: Basic Books.

Pryor, Frederic L. 1977. *The origins of the economy: A comparative study of distribution in primitive and peasant economies*. New York: Academic Press.

———. 1985. The invention of the plow. *Comparative Studies in Society and History* 27:727–43.

Roberts, D. F. Body weight, race, and climate. *American Journal of Physical Anthropology* 2 (1953): 553–558.

Rohner, Ronald P., Billie R. DeWalt, and Robert C. Ness. 1973. Ethnographer bias in cross-cultural resesarch: An empirical study. *Behavior Science Notes* 8:275–317.

Rohner, Ronald P., and Evelyn C. Rohner. 1981. Assessing interrater influence in cross-cultural research: A methodological note. *Behavior Science Research* 16:341–51.

Romney, A. Kimball, Susan C. Weller, and William H. Batchelder. 1986. Culture as consensus: A theory of culture and informant accuracy. *American Anthropologist* 88:313–38.

Rosenthal, Robert. 1966. *Experimenter effects in behavioral research, enlarged edition*. New York: Irvington.

Rosenthal, Robert, and L. Jacobson. 1968. *Pygmalion in the classroom*. New York: Holt, Rinehart and Winston.

Rosenthal, Robert, and Ralph L. Rosnow. 1984. *Essentials of behavioral research: Methods and data analysis*. New York: McGraw-Hill.

Ross, Marc Howard. 1983. Political decision making and conflict: Additional cross-cultural codes and scales. *Ethnology* 22:169–92.

Seligman, C. G., and Brenda Z. Seligman. 1932. *Pagan tribes of the Nilotic Sudan*. London: George Routledge & Sons.

Senter, R. J. 1969. *Analysis of data: Introductory statistics for the behavioral sciences*. Glenview, Ill.: Scott Foresman.

Siegel, Sidney. 1956. *Nonparametric statistics for the behavioral sciences*. New York: McGraw-Hill.

Stout, David B. 1947. *San Blas Cuna acculturation: An introduction*. New York: Viking Fund Publications in Anthropology.

Tatje, Terrence A. 1970. Problems of concept definition for comparative studies. In *A handbook of method in cultural anthropology*, ed. Raoul Naroll and Ronald Cohen, 689–96. Garden City, N.Y.: Natural History Press.

Tatje, Terrence A., and Raoul Naroll. 1970. Two measures of societal complexity: An empirical cross-cultural comparison. In *A handbook of method in cultural anthropology*, ed. Raoul Naroll and Ronald Cohen, 766–833. Garden City, N.Y.: Natural History Press.

Textor, Robert B., compiler. 1967. *A Cross-Cultural Summary*. New Haven, Conn.: HRAF Press.

Tylor, Edward B. 1889. On a method of investigating the development of institutions applied to the laws of marriage and descent. *Journal of the Royal Anthropological Institute of Great Britain and Ireland* 18:245–72.

Villaverde, Juan. 1909. The Ifugaos of Quiangan and vicinity. Translated, edited, and illustrated by Dean C. Worcester. With notes and an addendum by L. E. Case. Philippine Journal of Science 4A:237–262 (HRAF Source 19 in the Ifugao file).

Weller, Susan C. 1998. Structured interviewing and questionnaire construction. In *Handbook of methods in cultural anthropology*, ed. H. Russell Bernard, 365–409. Walnut Creek, Calif.: AltaMira Press.

White, Douglas R. 1990. Reliability in comparative and ethnographic observations: The example of high inference father-child interaction measures. *Journal of Quantitative Anthropology* 2:109–50.

Whiting, Beatrice B., ed. 1963. *Six cultures: Studies of child rearing*. New York: Wiley.

Whiting, Beatrice B., and Carolyn P. Edwards. 1973. A cross-cultural analysis of sex differences in the behavior of children aged three through eleven. *Journal of Social Psychology* 91:171–88.

Whiting, Beatrice, and John Whiting. 1970. Methods for observing and recording behavior. In *A handbook of method in cultural anthropology*, ed. Raoul Naroll and Ronald Cohen, 974–89. Garden City, N.Y.: Natural History Press.

———. 1975. *Children of six cultures*. Cambridge: Harvard University Press.

Whiting, John W. M. 1954. Methods and problems in cross-cultural research. In *Handbook of social psychology*, ed. Gardner Lindzey and Elliot Aronson. Reading, Mass.: Addison-Wesley.

———. 1981. Environmental constraints on infant care practices. In *Handbook of cross-cultural human development*, ed. Ruth H. Munroe, Robert L. Munroe, and Beatrice B. Whiting, 155–79. New York: Garland.

Whiting, John W. M., Irvin L. Child, William W. Lambert et al. 1966. *Field Guide for a Study of Socialization*. New York: Wiley.

Whyte, Martin K. 1978. Cross-cultural studies of women and the male bias problem. *Behavior Science Research* 13:65–80.

Witkowski, Stanley R. n.d. Environmental familiarity and models of band organization. Unpublished manuscript. New Haven, Conn.: Human Relations Area Files.

Zeller, Richard A., and Edward G. Carmines. 1980. *Measurement in the social sciences: The link between theory and data*. New York: Cambridge University Press.

Index

Page numbers in italic refer to figures or tables.

Index

About the Authors

Carol R. Ember (Ph.D. Harvard University, 1971) is executive director of the Human Relations Area Files, Inc. (HRAF), an international not-for-profit research agency at Yale University that produces annual installments of the electronic Collection of Ethnography and the electronic Collection of Archaeology. She has served as president of the Society for Cross-Cultural Research and serves on the boards of three journals: *Cross-Cultural Research*, *Ethos*, and *Journal of Conflict Resolution*. She has received grants (with Melvin Ember and Bruce Russett) from the National Science Foundation and United States Institute of Peace to support her research on war and interpersonal violence. Ember has recently received grants (with Robert Munroe and Michael Burton) from NSF to support the Summer Institutes for Comparative Anthropological Research. She has conducted cross-cultural research on variation in family, kinship, and gender roles, and cross-species research on female-male bonding and female sexuality. She is the senior author of *Anthropology, 10th Edition* (Prentice Hall, forthcoming) and *Cultural Anthropology, 10th Edition* (Prentice Hall, forthcoming). Ember is coeditor of *Countries and Their Cultures* (Gale/Macmillan, forthcoming) and the *Encyclopedia of Urban Cultures* (Scholastic/Grolier, forthcoming).

Melvin Ember (Ph.D. Yale University, 1958) is president of the Human Relations Area Files, Inc. and editor of *Cross-Cultural Research*, the official journal of the Society for Cross-Cultural Research. He directed the first NSF Summer Institute in Cross-Cultural Research in 1964 and served as president of the Society for Cross-Cultural Research. He is coeditor of the *Encyclopedia of Cultural Anthropology* (Henry Holt,

1996), *American Immigrant Cultures* (Macmillan, 1998), and the *Encyclopedia of Prehistory* (Kluwer/Plenum, forthcoming), *Countries and Their Cultures* (Gale/Macmillan, forthcoming) and the *Encyclopedia of Urban Cultures* (Scholastic/Grolier, forthcoming). His cross-cultural research has been supported by NSF, the National Institute of Mental Health, and the U.S. Institute of Peace, and has focused on marital residence, marriage, family and kinship, war and peace, and interpersonal violence. He is coauthor (with Burton Pasternak and Carol R. Ember) of *Sex, Gender, and Kinship: A Cross-Cultural Perspective* (Prentice Hall 1997).